MALICE IN WONDERLAND

Other Books

For the Law Student

The Art of the Law School Transfer: A Guide to Transferring Law Schools

Later-in-Life Lawyers: Tips for the Non-Traditional Law Student

Law School Fast Track: Essential Habits for Law School Success

Law School: Getting In, Getting Good, Getting the Gold

Law School Undercover: A Veteran Law Professor Tells the Truth About Admissions, Classes, Cases, Exams, Law Review, and More

Planet Law School II: What You Need to Know (Before You Go)— but Didn't Know to Ask…and No One Else Will Tell You

The Slacker's Guide to Law School: Success Without Stress

For the New Lawyer

The Insider's Guide to Getting a Big Firm Job: What Every Law Student Should Know About Interviewing

Jagged Rocks of Wisdom: Professional Advice for the New Attorney

Jagged Rocks of Wisdom—The Memo: Mastering the Legal Memorandum

Jagged Rocks of Wisdom—Negotiation: Mastering the Art of the Deal

Jagged Rocks of Wisdom—Contracts: Mastering the Art of Contract Drafting (forthcoming)

The Young Lawyer's Jungle Book: A Survival Guide

Non-Law Adventures

College Fast Track: Essential Habits for Less Stress and More Success in College

Grains of Golden Sand: Adventures in War-Torn Africa

Training Wheels for Student Leaders: A Junior Counseling Program in Action

MALICE IN WONDERLAND

WHAT EVERY LAW STUDENT
SHOULD HAVE FOR THE TRIP

THADDEUS HATTER

THE FINE PRINT PRESS

HONOLULU

Recognition is owed to Charles Lutwidge Dodgson, as Lewis Carroll, author of *Alice's Adventures in Wonderland,* published in 1865. The quotes, references, parody, and allusions are to Alice and the characters in *Alice's Adventures in Wonderland.*

Published by
The Fine Print Press, Ltd.
Honolulu, Hawaii
Website: www.fineprintpress.com
Email: info@fineprintpress.com

Library of Congress Cataloging-in-Publication Data

Hatter, Thaddeus, 1983-.
   Malice in wonderland: what every law student should have for the trip /
      Thaddeus Hatter.
   p. cm.
ISBN 978-1-888960-91-4 (softcover : alk. paper) 1. Law students--United
States. 2. Law--Study and teaching--United States. I. Title.
   KF283.H38 2012
   340.071'173--dc23

                         2012014657

Cover design and typesetting by Designwoerks, Wichita, Kansas.

The text face is Esprit Book, designed by Jovica Veljović and issued by ITC in 1985; supplemented with chapter headings in Castellar, designed by John Peters and issued by Monotype in 1957, section headings in Poppl-Laudatio, designed in 1982 by Friedrich Poppl for the H. Berthold AG Typefoundry of Berlin, and accent uses of American Typewriter, Helvetica Neue, Law & Order, and Old English.

PRINTED IN THE UNITED STATES OF AMERICA
20 19 18 17 16 15 14 13 12   9 8 7 6 5 4 3 2 1

Contents

DEDICATION

This book is dedicated to my parents, Jane and John. Being your son is a blessing. You are my heroes.

And to Uncle Steve, without your ferocious encouragement, I doubt that I would have seen this through. Thank you for helping open my eyes to Wonderland.

And finally some wisdom to live by from my favorite band of "Mad Hatters":

> *There is a road, no simple highway,*
> *Between the dawn and the dark of night*
> *And if you go, no one may follow,*
> *That path is for your steps alone*

—Grateful Dead

ACKNOWLEDGEMENTS

To Mom, my first and fiercest editor. You read every draft and guided me the whole way. I could not have done it without you.

To Dad, your unwavering support and supreme confidence in me are the greatest gifts I have ever received.

To my sister, who was my chief media strategist. Thank you for your support and for taking your job seriously.

To Daniel, you gave the book serious attention; it is better because of your review.

To EJ, my junior media strategist.

To the faculty and staff at Washington University School of Law, thank you for providing me with a great legal education. You are true professionals.

To Mr. Dee and Dr. Sandler, you are two of the greatest writing teachers anywhere; thank you for sharing your wisdom.

To Thane Messinger, who journeyed to Wonderland in the distant past, who offered a literary twist on a singular story, and who helped bring the story to life. Thank you for taking a chance. You are one enlightened cat.

To Winnie and Bruno, you are both a part of me.

"But I don't want to go among mad people," Alice remarked.

"Oh, you can't help that," said the Cat: "We're all mad here. I'm mad. You're mad."

"How do you know I'm mad?" said Alice.

"You must be," said the Cat, "or you wouldn't have come here."

—Charles Lutwidge Dodgson, writing
under the pseudonym Lewis Carroll,
from *Alice's Adventures in Wonderland*

THE TRIP

amazon.com

**Karen Brady
has sent you a gift.**

Saw this article by a Wash U law
grad & he wrote this book. Looks
like it has lots of useful tidbits.
Enjoy! Love, mom & dad

Included with Malice in Wonderland: What Every Law Student
Should Have for the Trip

Your order of October 11, 2012 (Order ID 105-4824192-9170662)

Qty.	Item
1	**Malice in Wonderland: What Every Law Student Should Have for the Trip** Thaddeus Hatter --- Paperback **(** P-1-U15C41 **)** 1888960914

This completes your gift order.

Have feedback on how we packaged your order? Tell us at www.amazon.com/packaging.

Returns Are Easy!

Most items can be refunded, exchanged, or replaced when returned in original and unopened condition.
Visit http://www.amazon.com/returns to start your return, or http://www.amazon.com/help for more
information on return policies.

Gift Cards
Millions of items. No expiration.
www.amazon.com/giftcards

– I –

WONDERLAND

It would be nice if something made sense for a change.

You are about to embark on a wild trip down the rabbit hole. When you emerge, you'll find yourself in a strange, unfamiliar "Wonderland:" Law School. Suddenly up is down, right is left, and north is south. Or east. Or west-southwest. Whatever. Everything you thought you knew about "school" is about to be flipped on its head.

How do I know this?

Not too long ago, I set out on the same trip, completely unprepared for what was in store. I knew nothing about case briefs, study groups, or outlining. I was not ready to deal with prickly professors, had no clue when or how to study law, and was shocked—appalled really,—to find out that there was homework due on the first day!

And this wasn't just any homework. It was massive, foreign, bizarre. The experience was surreal—as if I would wake up and be back in the familiar world of easy classes, nice professors, and good times. But there was no waking up; the trip would go on and on and on. I felt like a guest at the Mad Hatter's tea party, with odd puzzles uttered at random..."Why is a raven like a writing desk?"

Sure, I had friends who tried to explain some of these law school mysteries. But every time they would start using alien terms like "fact-pattern," "Rule 12(b)(6)," or "appellate brief," my eyes glazed over and my thoughts wandered to more important things (...In the song *Blinded by the Light,* are they singing "wrapped up like a *'douche'*" or "revved up like a *'deuce'*"...what the Hell is a deuce?...who says that anyway?? I wonder if I can get a deal on a weekend to Vegas.)

And you can forget about discussing the "law school experience" (pretentious air quotes included) with anyone over the age of 40. Every time I had to hear, "…well, back when *I* was in law school, we didn't even *have* computers—we actually had to go the library and do everything…by…hand!" I imagined that being waterboarded would be a more pleasant way to spend ten minutes. Yes, they may have actually gone to law school, and they may have actually practiced law for years, and they may actually have been right. But if I had to listen to one more graying Baby Boomer wax nostalgic for the days of oil lamps and parchment paper, I was going to shoot myself…with one of their muskets.

When it came to discussing law school, I guess that you could say that I chose the blue pill. I was perfectly content to continuing wandering around in a sweet state of ignorant bliss. Maybe I was in denial about the volume of work that was in store, or maybe I convinced myself that I would magically figure everything out, or maybe I just didn't want to think about it. Whatever the reason, I went into my first year cold turkey, armed with as little information as humanly possible. Make no mistake: this hurt. I suffered some *serious* bumps, which I will recount here for your entertainment and hopefully, your education.

After spending several months in a dense cloud of stress and bewilderment, I gradually emerged from the ether and started to make sense of the vexing mysteries of law school. I figured out what a case brief was, how long it should take, and what parts were truly important. I discovered what it meant to "outline" and why people do it. And I finally learned how to calmly deal with that terrifying moment at 8:01 a.m. in Torts when, after a long night of Ketel One and karaoke, you hear the eight most dreaded words in your first year of law school: "Mr. (or Ms.) [your name here], would you explain to the class…."

Slowly, everything became less foggy, the seasons changed, and I managed to make it through my first year. My second and third years each went more smoothly, and by the time graduation rolled around, I was finally dancing to the right rhythm of the law school beat. But parts of that first year were inefficient and needlessly stressful. With the right advice, the first leg of my trip would have been a lot more productive, and more importantly, a lot more fun.

– II –

UNCLE

"Cheshire Puss…would you tell me please, which way I ought to go from here?"

As I sat marinating in my sumo-sized, polyester robe well into the 15th hour of the commencement ceremony, my mind began to wander back to those first few months. Wow, was I a mess. It made me shudder to think of all the things I had been doing wrong and had wasted time worrying about. Then, suddenly…it hit me square in the back of the head. (The jolt actually may have come from my friend in the row behind me suggesting that I wake up for the degree awarding ceremony.) You know the old saying, "lightening striketh ye in mysterious ways…" No really, I am pretty sure someone said that. I think it was Mark Twain. Or maybe Gary Busey.

If only someone had sat me down, cut through the customary pretense and bullshit, and just *told me what I really needed to know,* I could have avoided much of the stress and headache I'd experienced.

I am not talking about the canned orientation spiel from a hoped-up admissions officer named Mandy who is one soy vanilla latte away from the legal limit. Nor did I need to sit through another afterschool-special monologue on the value of a quality legal education from a prehistoric judge named Arthur Cobblepott III, whose tenure on the bench predated the polio vaccine. And I certainly had my fill of riveting Q&A sessions with argyle-clad rising 3Ls named Randolph or Chip, who loved to brag about how they managed to snag a "big law" job. (Keep that collar popped, buddy, you look good.) I suffered through enough of these lectures. None of them accomplished what they were supposed to. None of them prepared me for law school.

What I really needed to get me ready for Wonderland was the *right* tour guide. What I needed was the cool uncle. You know the one. The uncle who fixes a speeding ticket without telling your parents. The uncle who taught you how to shoot tequila on your 19th…*er*, 21st birthday. The uncle who never wastes time telling you what he thinks you are supposed to hear, but who tells you what you actually need to know. He doesn't have all the answers, nor will he solve every one of your problems. But he will level with you, he has your best interests at heart, and he will do everything in his power to make your life better (and more fun).

I thought to myself: surely there must be a reference book out there that fits this description. After all, the canon of literary works describing, explaining, dissecting, and critiquing the law school experience is vast and filled with all kinds of treatises. Surely the cool uncle of law school literature already exists. I just never found him, right?

But after spending countless hours *(okay, three hours)* in libraries and bookstores *(okay, a Barnes and Noble up the street)* perusing all of the titles that I could get my hands on *(okay, the first four books I picked off of the shelf)*, I began to doubt whether such a book actually existed. Was the cool uncle of law school literature just a myth? Was Wonderland missing its real tour guide?

As my search deepened *(okay, by the second book)*, something became startlingly apparent about the books written for 1Ls: curling up with one of these little gems was only slightly more enjoyable than passing a kidney stone. And just to pour kosher salt in the wound, most of these masterworks are about 4,500 pages long. The prospect of spending the few last sacred days of freedom lounging by a pool reading the *Encyclopedia of Law School: 1500 pages of everything you ever needed or wanted to know about law school…ever…and More!* was an excruciating thought.

As I probed deeper still *(the third book)*, I uncovered another troubling reality: first year law books are overloaded with too much information! Do I really need to read a 15-page dissertation on the evolution of the English Common Law before I have received my orientation schedule? Is it necessary for me grasp

the detailed mechanics of appellate brief writing before I actually know what a brief is? Or a case? Or a citation?! I began to think that most rising first years may be more nervous about starting law school *after* finishing one of these lengthy tomes than before they started.

And while the books that I came across were certainly heavy on academic information, they were *devoid of practical, real-world advice!* The first year is about more than just homework and exams. Dealing with professors and interacting with classmates presents a whole new set of challenges that requires some serious *'splainin'*, Lucy.

Three-quarters of the way through the fourth book, my left upper lip began to quiver uncontrollably. My body was rejecting this material. It looked like a bad Elvis impersonator was stuck in the law school reference section. I had to get out of there. I beelined out of the bookstore and made a mad dash to the nearest pub where I immediately downed two large shots of straight gin and demanded that the barkeep—I think his name was Sam Malone—give me the Chinatown special and smack me in the face until I came to my senses.

As I sat alone in that empty bar (it was 10:15 a.m.), hunched over the counter, ice pack pressed against my swollen cheek, I knew that something had to be done. Granted, I didn't read every law book found in the Amazon catalog, but I had a hunch that they all suffered from the same set of problems: boring, *waaay* too much unnecessary information, boring, bad advice, and boring. Incoming first years deserved better. They needed someone to rescue them from the doldrums of 1L reference book purgatory. 1Ls were descending down the rabbit hole, alone, in the dark, without anyone to shine a light down that tunnel.

Until now. Please allow me to you introduce you to the Cool Uncle you didn't know you needed and never knew you had. Meet your *Uncle Malice*.

Above ground I go by my proper name, Thaddeus Hatter. (That's what everyone expects, and who am I not to give it to 'em?) Yet here in Wonderland, I'm just Uncle Malice.

In the coming pages, you are going to get tips and advice that I guarantee you will not get anywhere else. Uncle Malice is going to guide you through Wonderland. By the time we are done, you'll know what case briefs are and how to prepare them, what it means to outline and how you should approach it, and what to expect during finals. The work you will have in law school is different from anything you have ever done before. That's why I am going to give you the most practical and important academic information without clouding your head with an excessive amount of trivial details. And the best part…it won't take 4,500 pages to do it.

That's not all Uncle Malice has for you. To be really prepared for those first few months, you will need to know the *truth* about class, professors, and classmates. But Uncle Malice wouldn't think of spoon-feeding you the fluff and propaganda that is forced down your throat in the first year reference books written by uptight, out-of-touch professors, stuck-up law graduates, or egghead lawyers.

In fact, books written by law school professors will *never* tell you the truth about how to deal with all the confusing new situations that you will soon face. It's like talking to your parents about sex. They'll try to act cool about the topic, but when it comes down to the real nitty-gritty, they aren't going to talk positions with you. Same with professors: they simply aren't going to tell you what you really need to know.

To be fair, some of the books written by former law students and practicing attorneys are helpful…if you are suffering from chronic insomnia. Enough first-year law school books are tailored for type-A overachievers who memorized Atticus Finch's closing argument in *To Kill in Mockingbird* when they were 8 years old and got their first subscription to *American Lawyer Magazine* on their twelfth birthday. Your Uncle Malice is not having any of it.

So let's get a few things straight right now—reading this book will not help you rank in the Top 10% of your class, land a job at a top firm, make law review, or pass the bar exam. If you are reading this because you hope it will quell your insatiable curiosity about moot court competitions, the student bar association, trial teams, or getting published before your 22nd birthday, kindly step away from the book, run to the nearest computer, and Google the following words: "rising 1L seeks professional help." I am not going to lecture you on how to start building the perfect résumé. Nor I am going to preach to you about the advantages of leaving your laptop at home during class. And I certainly won't waste your time with twenty-five pages on the history and educational philosophy behind the Socratic Method.

But I will tell you what to do when your Contracts teacher, Professor McNasty, indulges his masochistic desires and treats you as his verbal punching bag with a series of questions that he might as well be asking in Farsi because it is 9:07 a.m., you are massively hung over, and you have not a read a single case assigned for that day. I will divulge the guerrilla tactics that can help you preemptively strike against your professor. I am going to walk you through a "Socratic Fire Drill" and show you how it can buy you time in class after you are called on but have not been paying attention. I will explain why you should never wear tacky Christmas sweaters to school, and cue you in on what behavior you should avoid if you don't want everyone in your class to stick little pins in a small stuffed replica of your body every time you speak.

And there is so much more. Confused about the cryptic law school-speak that you will suddenly be hearing every day... "Gunner," anyone? Is "Lexis" a new car with a bad proofreader? Not sure what a "study group" is and whether you have to join one? You have to come to the right place. What follows is the advice and explanations that I wish someone had given me, delivered in a way that would actually have kept my attention.

The first few months of law school can be a mess if you don't have someone to show you the ropes. But don't worry, Uncle Malice has got your back. We'll do this together. So, kick off your moccasins, saddle in, and brace yourself for the trip...'cause after you take the red pill, Kansas goes bye-bye.

– III –

YOUR FIRST DAY

"Where shall I begin, please your Majesty?" he asked.
"Begin at the beginning," the King said gravely, "and go
on till you come to the end: then stop."

Butterflies in your stomach, the musty smell of decomposing library books, and a spread of stale croissants can mean only one thing: the first day of school. Yes, everyone reading this has danced the first-day tango numerous times. But first days in law school are different from what you have experienced in the past for one crucially important reason: *homework.* Pay close attention to what I am about to say: no matter what law school you will attend, there is almost a 100 % chance that you are going to have homework due on the first day of class, for *every class.* For those of you already aware of this barbaric rite of legal passage—*mazel tov.* I, on the other hand, was completely oblivious.

Like many first year students who go to law school straight from college, I was still in undergraduate mode. In college, as many of you will fondly remember, attending the first week of classes is almost an optional activity. The first day for the semester always followed the same familiar, happy routine: professors would offer a congenial welcome to their students, leisurely go over the syllabus, then adjourn class at least a half-hour early.

I was one of those people who needed to be gently eased back into school mode at the start of each semester, and found this to be a comforting ritual. If the class was held sometime after 1:00 p.m., I may have even left the sanctuary of my twin water bed (very popular with the ladies) to attend this dog and pony show. Over the course of my four years in college, I grew quite fond of this routine and had no reason to expect that law school professors would break rank with this hallowed collegiate tradition.

Thus, you can imagine how quickly my genuine surprise turned into sheer terror when Professor Von Torment strutted into Legal Practice class on day one, glanced down at his roll sheet, and singled out one of my unwitting classmates for a Socratic cavity search. No cozy introduction, no colorful PowerPoint presentation, no warm milk or cookies. Instead, Von Torment jumped right into the material (the actual...course...material!), and this unfortunate soul had the unenviable distinction of being the first person to speak in the first class on the first day. The Professor played Ike to this poor schmuck's Tina. Von Torment slammed him with detailed questions about the case that we had, apparently, been assigned to read.

For the next fifty minutes of class, I felt like Hunter S. Thompson on the tail end of a three-day bender. My face got flush, my hands became sweaty, and I started to hear a deep baritone voice in my head that soundly eerily similar to Morgan Freeman mocking me for being such a slacker. Trust me, you don't want Morgan Freeman in your head.

Thinking that the first day was going to be a veritable lovefest, I not only had failed to read the homework assignment, but I had also made a conscious decision to leave the textbook in my car. I remember thinking, "Why would I need books on the first day?! We'll go around the room, say where we are from, tell the class one interesting fact about ourselves, and then be dismissed early to frolic in the quadrangle like wild gazelle."

The scenario I envisioned was not what actually unfolded. Von Torment continued to grill this poor, unsuspecting soul while the rest of us did our best to keep still in order to avoid the Professor's Socratic sonar. I begged the law school deities to spare me the humiliation I would suffer should my name be next on the Professor's hit list. Fortunately, it wasn't my time. But that didn't stop Morgan Freeman from continuing to berate me with insults for the rest of class. (To this day, I cannot watch *Driving Miss Daisy* without breaking into a cold sweat.)

You should take away two key points from this anecdote. First, I can almost guarantee that *there is going to be homework due on the first day of class.* Find out what it is and do it. You may find a syllabus on the course website, or there may be a handout that you were supposed to pick up. Either way, figure it out, do the work, and be prepared from day one.

There is chance that your professor will use the first class to give a rambling monologue about the class curriculum and will delay the Socratic mind torture until the second day. But...not likely. Please don't risk it. There are going to times you go to class unprepared; it is a fact of life in law school. Just don't let it be *you* on the first day.

Second, bring your books to class even if you have not read the material. It makes you look prepared even when you aren't. A law student with no books stands out like Ted Nugent at a PETA rally. In fact, you should bring books even if they are not the right books; they will serve as an invaluable prop throughout your law school career. Without them, you are naked and will be a sitting duck.

Which brings me to another first-day gaffe that 1Ls fall victim to every year: the infamous cell-phone blunder. In every class, there is always one student who forgets to switch his or her phone to vibrate. Like clockwork, ten or fifteen minutes into the first class that student will get a call. Perhaps it is your mom wishing you good luck on the first day, your loving spouse phoning to say that they are thinking about you, or the random hookup that you had during orientation week letting you know that they found one of your socks wedged in their pillow case.

As soon as that person hits the green Call button, your phone is going to start blowin' up. You are going to reach for the wrong pocket, and when you finally get the right one (after making a lot of noise), you won't be able to locate the right button to turn off the #@^&! ringer. Your flailing arms and spastic gestures will cause quite a ruckus. And while you are frantically hurrying to silence the call, the entire class will come to a screeching halt as everyone gets to demo your new ringtone: Blondie's *I touch myself,* which you downloaded last Saturday at 2:30 a.m. after a particularly lonely evening. *"I don't want anybody else...when I think about you I touch myself....*" Take note ladies: quieting the mad ringing is more challenging for you because you have a propensity to bury your phones under a giant maze of "lady" things in your purse.

While your classmates get a kick out of the musical interlude, Professor de Devilish will not. Ring-Gate is going to put you on the Prof's radar early in the game. So remember to muzzle your phone before the first class and save yourself the unwanted attention.

Carrots from Uncle Malice

- Plan on having homework due for *each* class on your first day. Check the course websites or ask your classmates. Find out what it is and get it done.

- Switch the celly to vibrate before taking your seat. Take us out, Debbie Harry..."*I love myself; I want you to love me / When I feel down I want you above me.... Oooh I don't want anybody else...Oh no, oh no, oh no....*"

– IV –

WORK

"Read the directions, and directly you will be directed in the right direction."

By now, you have probably heard countless horror stories about the massive amounts of work assigned in the first year of law school. Sensational tales of back-to-back all-nighters, caffeine-fueled cram sessions, and 4:00 a.m. computer freezes are recycled every Fall and seem to grow in legend with each passing year. I will level with you: the first year *is* challenging and you *will* spend a *lot* of your time studying.

But with the right mindset and preparation, it does not have to be as bad as legions of past law students make it out to be. One of the major reasons that many 1Ls find the work so time-consuming is because it is completely different from anything that they have ever done before. That is where I come in. I wasted countless hours during my first few months doing unnecessary work because in an effort to be overly thorough, I spent *waaay* too much time…on the wrong things.

I don't want you to suffer the same experience. That is why I am going to help you navigate the homework labyrinth. Unfortunately, I know of no secret Jedi shortcuts that will reduce your homework load by 90%. Be wary of anyone who says that they do. But I *will* give you some hyper-practical advice that will allow you to cut out the extraneous work and focus more energy on the important stuff. The best students don't waste time on worthless crap.

In many ways, law school homework is both a blessing and a curse. It's a blessing because, with few exceptions, you never have to turn in written work on a regular basis. The majority of the assigned homework in the first year involves reading cases.

This means that when you do your homework (or even *if* you do your homework) is entirely up to you. Some students follow the syllabus religiously—and always read and brief cases before the day that the work is assigned. Good for them. Other students designate one or two days a week as their study days and spend several hours finishing their work on those days. The point is that without the nagging requirement of daily written homework hanging over your head, you will have freedom—pretty much total freedom—to design a routine that works best for you.

On the other hand, this sweeping autonomy can be a curse for students who tend to procrastinate or have difficulty following a disciplined schedule. My advice to you is to *force* yourself to maintain a routine and stay current. Do not get behind. Trust me, it's easy to happen, and the further behind you fall, the worse it gets. You don't want to pull a George Michael and get caught with your pants down in late November by coming to the startling realization that you have 250 pages of reading to catch-up on—for each course. This will not make for a pleasant Thanksgiving.

The unsettling thought of being called on when you are unprepared might provide a compelling incentive, but it shouldn't be your primary reason for keeping up with the work. You want to keep up with the work because it will make your life appreciably easier come exam time. If you keep up with your work, you will follow and understand class discussions. If you follow class discussions, you won't have to cram tons of information at the end of the semester. By not having to cram tons of information, scrounge for notes, or learn complicated legal doctrine for the first time, you will cut your stress level in half, or more.

The chronic procrastinators who don't heed this advice and fall way behind won't be so fortunate. You will spot them easily. Toward the end of the semester they begin to look like meth heads who have exhausted their supply. The worst can be found sitting Indian-style in the corner of the library taking apart laser disc players. You don't want to look like a meth head. Find a

schedule that works best for you and *make* yourself stick to it. Come finals, you will be very glad that you did.

BOXERS OR BRIEFS?

You are probably going to spend more time during your first year briefing cases than doing any other type of work. First the bad news: briefing cases is only slightly more fun than an ice-cold enema. When you first start, it will feel painfully time-consuming and tedious. Now the good news: by the end of this chapter, you will understand what a case brief is, why it is important, and how you should think about and prepare briefs. When we are done, you will have a clear idea how to capture the important details of a case without wasting hours focusing on the minutiae.

BASIC TRAINING

A case brief is a written summary of a case.

As you may or may not know, the overwhelming majority of your homework for your core first year classes (torts, contracts, property, criminal law, constitutional law, civil procedure, and at some schools, evidence) is reading cases. When a professor assigns a case, what they are assigning is the *written opinion* issued by the court for that particular case. For example, if your contracts teacher assigns *Kardashian v. Dignity,* you will read the opinion of the court that decided the case. Cases you'll read could be from the 1800s, or, in the case of an actual Kardashian, it could be from last week.

The purpose of a case brief is three-fold: First, it forces you to organize your notes on a case in a concise and consistent manner. Second, it gives you a reference in class when you are called on and asked to explain a case. Third, case briefs provide a study aid if you review cases that you read earlier in the semester.

Typically, case briefs include five sections: (1) procedural history; (2) facts; (3) legal issue(s); (4) holding (*i.e.,* decision) of the court; and (5) the court's rationale for its holding. The case name—*e.g., Joan Rivers v Gravity*—is the heading. Under or next to *Joan Rivers v Gravity* you write the date of the decision and the court that issued it. (For finals, you almost never need to know the date or name of the issuing court, but it may help you organize your notes. The exception is in Con Law, where case names are shorthand for the legal doctrine.) We will discuss finals in more detail in a bit.

I'll give you a synopsis of each section of the case brief and then I'll give you the juicy secrets that you need to make briefing a less painful exercise, even for our right-brained friends. A quick word to the wise: the rest of this section is by far the driest and densest stuff will we cover. I included it because I think it is an important part of the first year and I want you to be familiar with briefing before your start. So bear with me for a few moments and we'll get back to the good stuff shortly.

PROCEDURAL HISTORY

This section of a case brief (sometimes "procedural history" and sometimes just "procedure") refers to the sequence of *rulings and motions* which brought the case to the court that is issuing the opinion. Most of the cases you will read during your first year are appellate decisions. That is, some lower court decided the case and one of the parties to the case appealed the decision to an *appeals court.* Hence the term *appellate decision.* Simple? Yes, mostly. But it can get tricky, especially when the parties are referred to with different terms, such as *cross-complainant* or *petitioner* or *intervenor* rather than *plaintiff.* It can be hard to remember who's on first. Most likely, you will be reading the decision issued by the court that heard the case on appeal.

A little example may help make this more clear: Christina sues Britney for stealing a bottle of hair bleach from Christina's secret bleach vault. Unable to settle out-of-court, the case goes to trial. The first court to hear the case (called the trial or lower court) decides in favor of Christina. Britney decides to appeal the decision, and an appellate court agrees to (or, in some cases, must) hear the appeal and listen to Britney's argument about what the lower court got wrong. The appellate court will then issue an opinion affirming, rejecting, or modifying the decision of the lower court, and will explain its reasoning (usually). The decision issued by the appellate court, *Aguilera v. Spears,* is what you will be assigned to read. It's the reasoning of that opinion that you'll be expected to understand.

Given the importance of bleach (or, more likely, the legal point at issue, such as "bailment" in property law), the case might go one step further, to the U.S. Supreme Court. If so, it's the same process—but there are three steps rather than two. (And at either appellate level the case might switch to *Spears v. Aguilera.)*

All that you need to write down for the procedure section is the sequence of motions and rulings that brought Britney's case to the appellate court. Generally, these are listed at the top of the appellate court's opinion, so that is the first place to look. Refer to the handy model brief on the next page to see what a typical procedure section might include.

This is a basic procedure section, by the way. Many cases will involve *many* more motions and rulings—most of which will be omitted from your reading. This makes it easier and harder. Easier because you only have to read 5 or 15 pages. (Well, only a little bit "easier," as this is 5 or 15 pages of *dense* text.) It's harder because the court is talking to lawyers (and, even more, to other judges), not to law students. The case thus assumes the reader understands the intricacies of this text *and* the missing links *and* the context .

Here is an important secret for your exam: the procedural history is usually unimportant. Don't waste your time trying to memorize obscure procedural history for, say, Torts cases. On the off chance that the procedural history is important, as can be the case in Constitutional Law, you will know. How will you know? There are two ways. First, if you're awake in class, you'll know because the professor will probably make it a topic of discussion. The second way you will know is because professional study references, such as commercial outlines and "canned" briefs, will discuss it. If the professor or the study aids highlight the procedural history, then you should assume that it is worth knowing.

If this is still a little hazy, don't worry. It takes time to get familiar with the terminology, but you will start to get the hang of it after the first few briefs.

FACTS OF THE CASE

The facts section of the brief is the part where you list the key facts involved in the case. In *Aguilera v. Spears,* the facts may be that Christina and Britney used to be BFFs (well, almost forever); Britney spent a significant amount of time at Cristina's house; Christina showed Britney the secret location of her bleach vault *and* where the key was; Britney was the only other person who knew where the key to the bleach vault was hidden; and Christina never authorized Britney to enter the bleach vault without her (Christina) being there.

In your brief, you write these facts down, either in bullet point form or in paragraph form. One of the most difficult parts of the facts section is figuring out which facts are important. Many cases are long, complex and will involve *lots* of facts. Don't get overwhelmed. It is not necessary to include every single fact in your brief. I did this when I first started, and it was a monumental waste of time. Just try to determine what facts seem most important to the outcome of the case and include those.

ISSUE

The issue section of the brief is generally a one-sentence question: what is the issue being decided by the court? When a case is heard on appeal, the appellate court does not review the entire case, or allow the parties to re-argue every fact. Instead, there are a limited number of issues that the appellate court will review— and they are looking not at "issues of fact" ("Did the defendant do x?"), which is the job of the trial court. Instead, the appeals

court is looking at issues of law: "Is this the right rule?" "Was it applied correctly?" and "Is there an exception that should be applied—or created?" For purposes of your first year, it will generally only be one or two major issues that you will be responsible for knowing. In your law school casebooks, the cases are usually condensed to a single issue.

In *Cristina vs. Britney,* the issue looks something like this:

> **Issue:** Whether showing another person (Britney) where a bleach vault is located, and where the key to a bleach vault is located, gives that person (Britney) <u>implied consent</u> to enter the bleach vault without authorization and take bleach out of the vault.

It is a good practice to get in the habit of phrasing your **issue** section with the same wording in *every* brief. Thus, always starting the **issue section** with "Whether..." is a good idea because this issue section will always present a question—the issue.

This section can be tricky because the most important issues before the court are not always glaringly apparent. But don't fret—in a minute I am going to tell you how to make identifying the key issue an easier task.

HOLDING

The holding is the answer.

If the issue was the one stated in *Cristina vs. Britney,* for example, the holding is:

> **Holding:** No. Merely showing another person where a vault and key are located *does not* give that person implied consent to enter or remove items from the vault.

You should get in the habit of starting the holding with "Yes" or "No," because the holding answers the question posed by the issue section. Note too that the point is to understand the broader point of law: it's not about just bleach, it's about the expectations of property interests as applied in any similar situation.

If you can identify the key issue, you will be able to figure out the holding, because the holding is the answer to the issue. Do not panic, however, if the holding is not immediately obvious—many cases you will read are complex, and it is not always clear what the court actually decided. If something seems confusing to you, it is almost certainly confusing to many of your classmates.

* * *

This leads to an important point that applies throughout your law school career: when (not if) you are feeling mind-numbingly confused and are convinced that you must be stupidest person in the history of law school, follow these three steps: (1) take a long, deep breath; (2) gently clear your throat; and (3) calmly read this poem...out loud:

JABBERWOCKY

'Twas brillig, and the slithy toves Did gyre and gimble in the wabe; All mimsy were the borogoves, And the mome raths outgrabe.

'Beware the Jabberwock, my son! The jaws that bite, the claws that catch! Beware the Jujub bird, and shun The frumious Bandersnatch!'

He took his vorpal sword in hand: Long time the manxome foe he sought—So rested he by the Tumtum gree, And stood awhile in thought.

And as in uffish thought he stood, The Jabberwock, with eyes of flame, Came whiffling through the tulgey wook, And burbled as it came!

One, two! One, two! And through and through The vorpal blade went snicker-snack! He left it dead, and with its head He went galumphing back.

`And has thou slain the Jabberwock? Come to my arms, my beamish boy! O frabjous day! Calloh! Callay! He chortled in his joy._

`'Twas brillig, and the slithy toves Did gyre and gimble in the wabe; All mimsy were the borogoves, And the mome raths outgrabe._

—Lewis Carroll

Okay. Now go back to the part of the case that was confusing, and see if it makes sense this time. Next to Jabberwocky, legalese is a picnic!

If it still seems confusing and complicated after the Jabberwocky trick, then I would bet dollars to donuts that most of your classmates don't know what the hell it means either. Judges write in Jabberwocky. Everybody around you is going to pretend that they know what the words mean, but in reality, most of them probably don't have the first damn clue. Occasionally, this confusion can include the professor—so forget getting clarity in class. In short, don't panic.

Still, pretending that this convoluted piece of legal doctrine doesn't exist will not make it go away. And you might just need to know it for the exam. So, put on your detective hat and do a little sleuthing. Consult your commercial outlines for an explanation you can follow. Discuss it with the professor after class and ask a specific question to clarify that point: "In a case involving diversity jurisdiction, does the Erie doctrine mean that...?" Be careful about asking your classmates, as they might be just as lost. With a little legwork, you can usually decipher the Jabberwocky.

We now return to our regularly scheduled programming...

Reasoning/Rationale: This is the last section of the brief and it is often the longest. Here, you write down the reasoning behind the court's decision. In the opinion, the court is going to give a *holding,* and is then going to (or is supposed to) explain why they reached that particular holding. You should know that these explanations are rarely straightforward or simple and they frequently shoot off in many directions—this is one reason the average law school classroom sometimes seems like a mad tea party.

There are consistencies among these rationales, however. This is very much what learning the law is all about—finding and figuring out these consistencies. For instance, it is common (and expected) for courts to support their decisions by citing past cases with similar facts, and then explaining how the current case is *similar to* or *different from* the prior case(s). And, of course, some cases have greater value: the higher the court, the higher the value; the closer the court, the higher the value. You will discuss this type of argument (or "rationale") in great detail in your various classes, but for our purposes, all you really need to know is that this is referred to as "precedent." In other words, a court is supposed to look to what other courts said in the past, and why, so that future litigants will know pretty much which way a future court is likely to rule.

In *Christina v. Britney,* the court may support its holding by noting that a long line of cases including *Idol v. Bowie, Bolton v Cyrus,* and *Simpson v. Moore* all support the legal rule that showing a friend where your bleach vault and key are located does not give that person implied consent to take bleach without asking. In the reasoning/rational section, you would mention and perhaps explain, briefly, why the court referenced these cases to support its decision in *Christina vs. Britney.*

Appellate courts especially will refer to "public policy" arguments in their reasoning to support a holding. For example, in *Christina v. Britney,* the court might reason that, due to the harmful effects that bleach has on the ozone layer, it is not good public policy to allow the unauthorized movement of bleach among capricious pop stars who change hair colors like most people change socks.

Note that it's not likely that every prior case is going to be exactly like the one the court must decide. So, Mr. Idol had a special microphone supply room, Mr. Bolton a hidden shoe room, and Ms. Simpson a hidden stash of conditioner and bleach (but with no key). Each case will be different—sometimes a little, sometimes a lot, sometimes just enough. The court will reason through how applicable are the facts (key or no key, secret or super-secret, hair product or something else of personal value...), and, sometimes, how wise is the rule that these cases signify.

Sometimes, the rule starts to seem wrong, and thus courts begin to diverge in their decisions. If enough courts agree with them (the rationale!), then there might be a new rule. At first, this will be a "minority rule"; if its reasoning is sound, it might become the "majority rule." When dealing with these cases, you'll need to know *both*—and you need to know why (rationales!) one is the majority and the other is the minority, *and* which way the law is trending (is the majority rule about to become the minority rule?), *and* which way your professor believes it should trend (*i.e.,* which rule does your professor believe is correct, and why?). It might sound complicated, but when you break it down logically, it starts to make more sense.

What you should ultimately remember is that the court is going to use arguments (*i.e.,* rationales) to support its reasoning. When you first start reading cases, it will probably be difficult for you to know which arguments are the most important for you to jot down in your brief. My advice is to go with your instincts and write down what seems most important. If a court repeats an argument or spends a lot of time discussing a certain case, chances are it was instrumental in its decision and you should include it. Like all aspects of briefing, this will get easier as you read more cases.

Remember that it takes time and practice to get comfortable briefing, but being familiar with the terminology and general concepts that we have just discussed will put you ahead of the game.

DEBRIEFING: THE FOUR COMMANDMENTS

Now it is time for the *debriefing.* These Four Commandments of briefing are highly confidential: you will never hear them uttered by any law professor. If you treat these three commandments as the gospel and let them guide your approach to briefing from day one, you will save yourself valuable time and energy and your briefs will be better for it.

Debriefing Commandment #1

1. THOU SHALT ask thyself one thing out loud after reading a case: "When I take the exam in [x] months, *'what will I need to remember from this case?'''* Thou shalt use thine brief to answer thy question.

Shocking as it may seem, every case that you read during your first year of law school has been assigned for a reason. Specifically, the cases that you read will all contain a **holding** that either affirms rejects, adds to, explains, and in some cases, creates a *law.* Not "the" law, but a specific legal point—a rule of law. The actual "law" contained in the case is crucial for you to identify. More correctly, it's not really "contained" in the case like soda inside a can. It's more like this: the case is an example of that law. Understand the example, and you understand the law. It's like saying "Pepsi" and everyone has an instant vision of a soda can.

Let's take a Contract Law case. Throughout your first semester, you are going to read dozens of cases in Contracts. Each one of these cases is going to tell you something specific about Contract Law.

For example, in the case of *Kirstie Alley v. Dunkin' Donuts,* the holding of the court is that a *mutual mistake between two contracting parties is a sufficient reason to invalidate a contract.* Or in *Bristol Palin v. Contraception,* the holding could be that an *offer is not deemed valid until it is communicated to the offeree.* Don't worry if these examples sound strange or don't make sense; I am including them to show you what a holding from a contract case might look like. Why? Because that holding is going to look very close to a specific legal point: a rule of law. And that rule of law is going to be exactly what you'll need to use for your law exam. (Note: not just *know*, but *use*; more on that later.)

Once you're actually in law school, you won't be so confused because the case is simply illustrating a very specific rule—a narrow point of law—such as "mutual mistake" or what constitutes a valid "offer."

Each of the fifty or sixty or eighty cases you will read during the semester will contain a holding similar in style to these. Taken together, *these holdings make up the body of Contract Law that you will be responsible for knowing on the exam.*

Come finals time, *you will be expected to <u>apply</u> these holdings to a new set of hypothetical facts* that your professor will give you on the test. Now you can see why the *issue* and *holding* components of your brief are so critical; you identify the *legal question(s) being considered (issue)* and *answered (holding)* in the case.

And that brings us back to Debriefing Commandment #1: To help you identify each issue and holding, after you finish reading every case, you should get in the habit of asking yourself, out loud: When I take the exam, *what will I need to remember from this case!*

This is not a question; it's a Commandment. If you're not forcing yourself to understand why you just read the case, then you're wasting your time. There is *always* a legal point to a case— especially one in a casebook. Figure out why you were asked to read that case.

Thus, if you're reading the case in October, you would ask yourself (out loud!), "In two months when I take the exam, what will I need to remember from this case?" The answer is nearly always...the *holding* of the case. While the sight and sound of you talking to yourself once every thirty-five minutes may cause concern amongst your loved ones, it will help.

Let's refer back to our *Christina v. Britney* example to see how this works. After reading about two ladies named Christina and Britney, you remember to ask yourself out loud: "When I take the exam in [x] months, *'what will I need to remember from this case?'*"

Okay. Question asked. What's the answer?

What do *you* think your answer should be for *Christina v. Britney?*

How about some hints? First, *you are not going to have to remember specific facts,* such as Christina and Britney used to be friends. The facts are going to change with every case and *almost never* are you expected to recount specific facts from past cases on an exam. Law exams are filled with bizarre fact patterns and improbable storylines with wildly unsympathetic characters. Each one- or two-page question is obscenely complex—on purpose. The Mad Hatter would be proud.

Similarly, *you will not be asked to restate the procedure* from *Christina v. Britney,* because, outside of Civil Procedure, this is not something professors ever test. [Disclaimer: I am only 99.9 % sure about this assertion. There is always a remote possibility that some rogue, depraved law professor, who perpetrates telemarketing scams on the elderly in his free time, will ask you to restate the procedure of some minor case.] Thus, while the *procedure* section will help familiarize you with the legal terminology pertaining to various aspects of the litigation process, it is not something that you will need to know for the final.

Additionally, while the rationale is crucial to helping you understand *why* a court came out a certain way, the specific reasoning for a case is not vital to know for exams. On the exam, you will be expected to apply your *own reasoning* to defend your answers. You should recognize that the better that you understand the court's reasoning for a given holding, the easier it will be for you to support your own arguments (with different facts!) on an exam. The main function of the *rationale* is to help you make sense of a court's holding.

The real reason that you read *Christina v. Britney* was so that you could learn the law, or the holding of the case. In *Christina v. Britney:*

Holding: No. Merely showing another person where a vault and key are located *does not* give that person implied consent to enter or remove items from the vault.

This is the holding of the case and you need to know it on the final because you will be expected to apply this holding to a different set of hypothetical facts.

Hence, remember that after you finish reading every case you should recite, out loud, the First Debriefing Commandment: "When I take the exam in [x] months, *'what will I need to remember from this case?'"* The answer to the question is always the holding, and this is what you need to make sure to get down.

One last thing. Because the **issue** and **holding** are so important, I suggest that in every brief you write in **BIG BOLD letters** under the case name what the **issue(s)** and **holding(s)** of the particular case were. You can update and revise these headings if you put down one **issue** or **holding** and subsequently discover in class that it was actually a different one(s). Clearly delineating the **issue** and **holding** of each case in your briefs will make your life much easier when you begin reviewing for finals because it will provide you with a quick and easy reference point: the key takeaway for each case. *Hallelujah!*

Debriefing Commandment #2

THOU SHALT NOT forsake thy brain: Never forget that when thoust is called upon in thy class, thy case brief will either be thine best friend or thine worst enemy—and probably the latter.

Aside from helping you systematically organize your notes about a case and study for finals, briefs can be a valuable tool when you get called on in class (which we will discuss in detail in the next chapter). On the other hand, if you rely on your brief too much or make it excessively detailed, your brief will burn you. Hell hath no fury like an overly convoluted brief.

Yes, even I, Uncle Malice, was nervous about being called on during first year. Consequently, I would compile *extremely* long briefs that included almost every piece of information from the case, no matter how insignificant. I figured that by preparing exhaustive briefs, I would be ready for whatever question Professor Voldemort chose to throw my way, because my über-briefs would contain the answer. An unpleasant experience in Torts during my first month of school proved my plan badly misguided.

My Torts section was relatively small—about 35 people—and by the third week of class, I was one of the few students who had not been called on. I knew that I would be up to bat soon, and so I thoroughly read every case assigned for the week and cranked out briefs on steroids. These briefs were seemingly more detailed than the actual cases in the texts.

When I marched into class on Monday morning, I felt invincible. As expected, my name was the first one called. Bring it on Professor Lucifer—want to know the middle initial of the judge who rendered the opinion in the lower court? Got it covered. What's that? You want to me to recite in reverse chronological order all the cases that the court used in its reasoning? Ready to Engage. Oh—you think you are going to stump me by seeing if I know the difference between the concurrence and the dissent? Please rise a little earlier, Madame. Locked and Loaded!

Unfortunately, before I was able to deliver my blindingly acute responses to any of those questions, Professor Lucifer instead led off with a more benign inquiry:

"Mr. Malice—what did the court decide in *Tyson v. Earlobe?*"

"Umm...*what??*"

"Professor L...Could you...please...*uhh*...repeat the...*ahh*...question?"

"Sure. What did the court decide in *Tyson v. Earlobe?*"

My mind went blank. I pressed my face against my computer and began frantically scanning my five-page brief for a clue—*any* clue—that could help me find the answer. How could this be happening?! I spent *hours* preparing this brief and writing down every little obscure factoid about the case but somehow I had failed to remember what the court actually decided?

To make matters worse, because my brief was so detailed and long, I could not locate anything that might have put me on the right track to finding the answer. The tension in the room mounted as the steady hum of laptops and the loud sighs of an annoyed professor made it almost impossible for me to concentrate. Feeling defeated, I threw in the white towel and begrudgingly admitted that I was "not really sure" what the answer was. Disgusted with my presence, Professor Lucifer shot me The Look, gave me three lashings, and ordered me to bed with no pudding.

This little tidbit should tell you a few things. First, don't be so focused on capturing everything little detail in your brief that you forget what the case was actually about. Too many first-year students get in the habit of mindlessly *transcribing* their briefs without really *thinking* about what they are writing. I know that I was guilty of this because I would simply go through the motions of copying paragraphs from the court's opinion *word for word* into my "briefs."

This passive style of briefing does not force you to engage with the material, and consequently, you will not remember anything about the case—or at least you won't remember anything important about the case, in any way that will be useful to you in the exam. It was for this very reason that I could not answer Professor Lucifer's *basic* question as to what the court had decided in the case.

One tip to help remedy this problem:

Practice writing the takeaways from the opinion *in your own words* rather than merely regurgitating the court's opinion verbatim in your brief. This will be challenging in the beginning, but over time, it will make it easier for you to digest the substance of the case and comprehend the important points.

Along these lines, you should keep in mind that the longer you brief is, the more difficult it will be for you to actually *use* it: to locate the relevant section when you are called on in class. When you review your brief in the comfort of your cozy apartment or home, everything will flow perfectly and make total sense. It is a much different story when you have 90 classmates and an impatient professor staring at you as you frantically race through your brief to locate the answer to a simple question. Not fun.

I am not recommending that you limit your briefs to a single paragraph, nor that you spend hours trying to condense them onto one page. When you read long or complex cases, it is inevitable that you will have to prepare longer briefs. But always remember that simple and concise briefs will be your friends when you are using them in class and studying for finals.

Furthermore, don't view your briefs as cheat sheets that will contain the answer to every possible question that a professor may ask. I distinctly remember believing that if I just typed out everything I possibly could, the professor would never be able to stump me because all the answers would be at my fingertips. This never turns out to be the case. While professors might certainly ask you to recite some of the more mechanical and concrete aspects of a case, such as the facts and procedure, you should expect that they will also challenge you with more abstract and open-ended questions.

For example, the professor may ask your whether you agree with the court's holding, why you think the that court came out the way it did, or ask you to make an argument in favor of an alternative ruling. For these discussions, you will have to think critically about the case rather than simply referring to your brief (or anything else that might be on your desk). Try not to become too dependent on the brief for the answers; these are issues *you* will have to think through.

Having your briefs with you in class should alleviate some of the stress of being called on, not make it worse. If you keep it simple, actively engage with the material by putting it in your own words, and don't rely too heavily on the brief for all the answers, your briefs will become a reliable and trusted comrade during class discussions.

Debriefing Commandment #3

> 3. THOU SHALT remember that thy briefs will never be graded. So thou shall work hard to keep thy OCD under control.

I can tell you with almost virtual certainty that none of your professors will ever have you turn in a brief for a grade. Ever. There is a slight chance that they may ask (or offer) to see one of your briefs early in the semester to make sure that you are on the right track, but they will probably just give you informal feedback—no grade. Consequently, you will be wasting a considerable amount of time if you spend an extra thirty minutes per night adjusting the sp acing, editingg grammare, and correcting your's syntax. Your briefs are for you and you alone—all that matters is that you are able to follow and understand them.

This does not mean that a disorganized brief is a good brief. It's not. If your briefs are neat, organized, and consistent, you will have an easier time using them in class and, more importantly, when you study for finals. I would be willing to make a large wager that there is a strong correlation between highly organized briefs and performance on the final exam. You should strive to be as organized as possible with your briefs, and with your work in general, because it will make your life much easier throughout the semester and during finals.

But there is a fine line between organization and neurosis. If you are spending significant amounts of time every day color-coding opinions by the same judges, adjusting the font based on the geographic location of the Court, or double and triple checking to make sure that none of your sentences end in prepositions, you have gone too far too. If your briefs begin with an acknowledgement section, are hand-written in calligraphy with a montblanc pen, or contain illustrations, then...up your dosage.

I recognize that my OCD brothers and sisters are going to struggle mightily with this concept, but you have to trust me. Spending hours concocting the world's most perfect brief may make you feel warm and fuzzy inside, but it will have *absolutely no effect* on your final grade. Time is a precious commodity during your first year of law school and if you will waste it if you obsess over the formatting and stylistic (*i.e.* trivial) components of your brief.

Your time is much better spent identifying and understanding the issue and holding of a case because that is what you will have to know for the exam. So, if writing in the passive voice makes your eye-lid spasm or misspelling the plaintiff's name will cause you to break out in a hives, then go ahead and do what you need to do. Otherwise, don't drive yourself nuts.

Debriefing Commandment #4

> 4. THOU SHALT not forget to see thy legal forest through thine briefing trees.

This is the most important briefing commandment of them all. Don't lose sight of the fact that briefing is merely a means to help you understand the case-law; it is not an end in and of itself. Too much precious energy and concentration is squandered in the rote preparation of briefs, *rather than trying to understand the law, the reasoning of the case, and why the case has been assigned.*

Law professors do a terrible job explaining this, and classroom discussions compound the problem. Each time a professor asks a student to recite the procedure from a case, it sends the message that the procedure section is actually an important part of the brief. It is not. Having superb procedure sections (or fact sections) in your brief *will score you no points on an exam.* Thus, if it takes you an hour to brief a case and you spent 15 minutes writing down and thinking about the procedure, you just wasted 14 minutes. The name of the appellate court, the name of the presiding judge, the procedure and the facts are all *briefing trees;* the issue, holding and reasoning/rationale are the *legal forest.* Don't spend your time wading through the trees: concentrate on the forest.

Use a case to learn a specific legal rule—don't worship the case itself.

BLAZE YOUR OWN TRAIL

As you get further into the semester, you may develop your own unique system of note-taking that works better for you than a traditional brief. Perhaps you like to organize your notes in a different way or maybe you retain the information better with a different layout. Maybe you like to set each outline to music. If you do find a technique or approach better suited to your style of learning, don't be afraid to use it. It is nowhere written in stone that you have to follow the standard briefing model just laid out.

The point is that the law is the law: these concepts should apply to whatever method you eventually decide to use. At the end of the day, you need capture the **issue** and **holding** of the case because that is what you are going to be tested on.

I would like to leave you with a beautiful piece from the book of *Brieferonomy, 2:1*:

"Go not forth hastily, my children, without understanding into thine strange land of briefing mayhem for thine knowledge shall yield a bountiful harvest. Amen.

Carrots from Uncle Malice

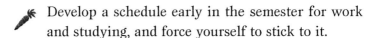 Develop a schedule early in the semester for work and studying, and force yourself to stick to it.

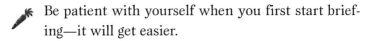 Be patient with yourself when you first start briefing—it will get easier.

 Follow the four debriefing commandments outlined above and you will make the most effective and efficient use of your precious time.

A MODEL CASE BRIEF

Christina v. Britney
123 U.S. 456 (2022)

Procedure:

- Plaintiff Christina accused Defendant Britney of stealing Christina's hair bleach from Christina's secret bleach vault

- Lower court ruled in favor of Plaintiff on all claims

- Defendant appealed, arguing that the trial court erred when it held that by showing Defendant where the bleach vault and key were located, Plaintiff had given implied consent to Defendant to enter the bleach vault and take her bleach

Facts:

- Christina and Britney were once best friends

- Britney spent a significant amount of time at Christina's house

- Christina showed Britney the secret bleach vault

- Christina showed Britney where the key to the bleach vault was hidden

- Britney was the only other person who knew where the key was hidden

Issue:

Does showing another person where a vault and key are located give that person an implied consent to take bleach out of the vault?

Holding:

No. Merely showing another person where a vault is located and where the key to the vault is located does not give an implied consent to take items from the vault.

Reasoning/Rationale:

- Precedent: The facts of this case are similar to established holdings in Idol v. Bowie, Bolton v. Cyrus, and Simpson v. Moore that giving a close friend access to your bleach vault does not give that friend implied consent to take bleach without asking

- Add'l Public Policy Rationale: Due to the harmful effects that bleach has on the ozone layer, it is not good public policy to allow the unauthorized movement of hair bleach among capricious pop stars who change hair colors like socks

Dissent (J. Lex): It is important to share and share alike. Sharing with friends is especially praiseworthy. Thus, the rule should be that long-term friendship creates an implied consent.

Dissent (J. Marx): The development of the proletariat is conditioned upon the development of the industrial bourgeoisie. No one should have more bleach than any other person; thus there should be no vaults; thus the law should recognize no property rights of any individual superior to any other. Bleachers of the world unite!

V

Professors

"I warn you dear child, if I lose my temper, you lose your head."

You may infer from the various nicknames I have given to law professors that they are a sadistic clique of devil-worshippers who were put on this earth to torment first-year law students. In reality, this is not the case. The overwhelming majority of professors in law school are thoughtful, reasonable people who genuinely love teaching.

As a group, law professors are accomplished law graduates who have a diverse set of experiences and backgrounds. I encourage you to cultivate relationships with the ones you like, and lean on them for guidance. Some of these relationships will last well past your three years.

Still, every law school will have at least a few professors who hate puppies or who tell four-year-olds that Santa Claus is make-believe. For whatever reason, they have made it their life's mission to intimidate and discourage every bright-eyed, bushy-tailed 1L they meet. If you are lucky, you won't run across too many of these irascible demon-people. But the odds are that you are going to have at least one. That's why in the next chapter, I am going to prepare you to deal with the worst of them.

There is one more important thing for you to keep in mind throughout the rest of our conversation: law professors are not there to spoon-feed you a bunch of legal rules for you to spit out come exam time. They are not going to write everything that you need to know for the test in succinct bullet points on the blackboard. They don't see that as their role. You shouldn't either. If you think you are going to do yourself any favors by furiously transcribing every word that comes out of the professor's mouth into a dense compendium of class notes, you are wrong. Mindless note-taking during class is a total waste of your time. The only thing it's good for is premature arthritis.

Instead, professors see themselves as your jousting partner; but instead of schooling you in hand-to-hand combat, they are going to attempt to condition your mind. Accordingly, professors generally provide fewer answers than questions, and they don't see it as their job to resolve every complex issue. Thus, to get the most out of class, you need to force yourself to meaningfully engage with the legal questions being raised.

In the following chapter, I am going to give you all the tips that you will need to make class more enjoyable and less stressful. But don't lose sight of the fact that at its core, a thoughtful class discussion is a live reenactment of what you will be expected to do on exams: apply legal reasoning to a complex set of facts that will not have definitive answers.

Carrots from Uncle Malice:

- Professors can be an invaluable resource; soak up their knowledge and foster lasting relationships.

- Don't let a few rotten apples ruin the harvest; bad professors are outliers. Be prepared.

VI

CLASS

"Who are you?" said the Caterpillar.

"I—I hardly know, Sir, just at present," Alice replied rather shyly, "at least I know who I was when I got up this morning, but I think I must have changed several times since then."

I distinctly remember: it was the last day before the end of the first semester. I was sitting in class counting down the final ten minutes until we were dismissed. I had not done the reading for class that day thinking that Professor McManiacal was going to go easy on us because it was the last day.

Wrong was I.

"Mr Malice. Would you be so kind as to explain the court's reasoning in *Sheen v. Tiger Blood?*"

[No case names were harmed during the writing of the book.]

I remember thinking, "C'mon man...are you *serious?* It's the last day and there are ten minutes left in class and you want to start with me *now??*"

Well, he *was* serious, and I was thus presented with a dilemma. Option A: I fold my cards and admit that I haven't the faintest idea about tiger blood or sheens thereto; or Option B: I go all-in and attempt to concoct a response that hits on at least some of the important points that Herr Professor had been discussing in class. I went with Option B.

I proceeded to let loose. Out of my mouth flew a convoluted, rambling string chalk full of key buzzwords that I hoped would make made me sound like I knew what the Hell I was talking about. As I listened to the words as they were coming out of my mouth, I realized that I sounded like Ozzy Osborne after three brimfuls of Merlot and a handful of Vicodin. But did I stop? Oh no. I kept digging deeper, hoping that somehow my disjointed, long-winded answer would eventually connect the right dots.

When I finally finished, Professor McManiacal took a deep breath, walked to the front of the class, paused for what seemed like an hour, then garbled a little "humph" under his breath. Had I done it? Did my verbose Hail Mary actually work? Had I pulled a 1L Kaiser Soze?

"Umm…Mr. Malice. That was…uhh…interesting. I would appreciate, and I think that the class would appreciate it as well, if you could repeat that answer…only this time, in English."

That, boys and girls, is what happens when you aren't prepared to deal with the trappings of the Socratic Method.

Fear not! This chapter will provide you with the strategies and insights to handle the myriad of precarious situations that all 1Ls will eventually find themselves in.

I LOVE IT WHEN YOU SOCRATES ME, BABY

The Socratic Method is the style of teaching used by law professors where a student is randomly selected to explain and defend various aspects of a court's decision. Sometimes these encounters last for as little as a minute; other times they can go on for an entire class.

The Socratic Method is supposed to force students to examine the assumptions underlying their arguments and challenge their thinking. Unfortunately, in many law schools, the original intent of the Socratic Method has been perverted by a cadre of law professors who employ the technique as a check on class preparedness rather than a critical thinking exercise. Regardless, it is going to be a big part of your first year.

Generally, once you have been picked on (or "picked off"), you can rest easy for a few weeks, because professors normally call on everyone at least once before returning the top of the order. However, there are exceptions, so you should make sure that your professor is not one of those wily creatures who will call on the same people two or three times before calling on other students once. If you are lucky, you will have at least one professor who calls on students in alphabetical order.

In your first few months, the omnipresent thought of being called on might be a source of anxiety. Many abhor the idea of speaking in front of a crowd and will dread going to class for this reason. Others take to it more naturally and relish the opportunity to spar with the professor in front of their peers. And the rest will lie somewhere in the middle; you won't really worry about it too much until you are the one summoned to speak. Whichever camp you fall into, the following advice is for you: *every* law school employs the Socratic Method during first-year, and everyone will have their number called at some point.

DON'T PULL A SALLY FIELD

All law students, no matter how sharp or how great in public speaking, will have at least one bad Socratic experience. The quicker you accept this, the better that you will deal with it when it happens. Every law graduate I know can recount some moment where they either got tongue-tied, blanked on an easy question, or gave a completely nonsensical answer. Even though it will seem agonizing at the time, within a day everyone will have forgotten because they will be too worried about being next. Law students have a short memory about these things and your gaffe will have a limited half-life.

Unless…you pull a Sally Field.

In 1985, Ms. Field won an academy award for best actress for the film *Places in the Heart.* Toward the end of her acceptance speech, she blurted out, "…I can't deny the fact that you like me right now, *you like me!*" Her acceptance became widely known as the "You like me, You *really* like me!!" speech, and it has been routinely mocked and lampooned ever since.

Out of the thousands of rambling, self-important Oscar speeches delivered over the Academy's history, Ms. Field's stands out because hers truly makes you *cringe.* This is exactly what you want to *avoid* when you are called on in class. Normally, screwups in class are like bad Oscar speeches: painful to endure when they happen, but quickly forgotten. However, if the cringe-inducing quotient of your back-and-forth with the prof exceeds the max threshold, your charade will grow to live in law school infamy.

Accordingly, here is a short, but by no means exhaustive, list of things that rank high on the cringe-meter that you should avoid doing when you are called on: bursting into tears and shrieking "but he told me he *loved me!*"; launching into your favorite Andrew Dice Clay routine; seizing the opportunity to filibuster the rest of the class with a political speech praising the virtues of peaceful resistance to armed conflict; informing the professor that he is "not the father;" responding to the professor, "why don't you have *your mother* recite the facts"; or blasting techno from your laptop while you do the worm all the way down the aisle. [Disclaimer: You might actually be able to pull this last one off if you have seriously sweet moves.] Doing any of the above will ensure that your episode will go down in the pantheon of famous Socratic meltdowns, a distinction I am sure you do not want.

DEFENSE IS THE BEST OFFENSE

As alluded to earlier, the majority of law professors are not evil, demented members of the occult whose main goal in life is to embarrass and humiliate you in front of your classmates. To the contrary, most professors are sensitive to the fact that not everyone feels comfortable speaking in front of large groups. You will have many nice teachers who will graciously help students by being patient and talking them through difficult questions when they sense that they are intimidated or nervous.

But there are a select few out there who will not be so kind. This bitter bunch of curmudgeons will cut you very little slack if you are struggling through an answer. That is why it is crucial that you know how to deal with them.

For starters, you should never do what I did and try to B.S. your way through an answer when you are dealing with an especially petulant professor. Maybe 1 out of 50 times you are going to get lucky and stumble upon the right answer. The other 49 times are going to leave you feeling that you just went through security with an overzealous TSA "officer." Your professor is going to sense right away that the emperor has no clothes and might see fit to use his bully-pulpit to give you a Socratic Shakedown in front of the class with even more difficult questions—which profs have on tap. (In the interest of gender equality, it could just as easily be a female professor who decides to unleash a Socratic bitch-slap.) It won't take long for you to say "uncle," at which point the professor will give you the proverbial "suck-it" gesture, light up a Virginia Slim 120, and proudly declare victory.

So what should you do if you find yourself in one of these situations? Two strategies are effective. First, if you come to class having not read and your professor is one of these incorrigible, heartless chaps who would love nothing more than to eat your lunch in front of the class, then you are better off to go up to him beforehand and inform him that you are unprepared. This can be a tough pill to swallow and he will probably scold you for your misfeasance, but at least you will have the peace of mind to know that you won't get called on. Probably. If you decide to take this approach, expect that you will become a marked man or woman; you should definitely be prepared to speak in upcoming classes.

In big classes, it will be tempting to not say anything to the professor and play the house odds that you won't get called on. With 80 or 100 or more students in a class, you might be able to escape unscathed. Then again, you might not. This is a personal decision and you will have to do a little cost/benefit analysis to determine whether the risk is worth taking. I can tell you that if you choose to roll the dice, each passing minute will feel like an eternity and every time the professor looks down at his roll sheet, your stomach will churn like Mt. Vesuvius.

If you decide to let it ride and the roulette wheel lands on your number, you are going to have to admit defeat and tell the professor that you are unprepared. This may seem like the only logical thing for you to do, but for some reason law students have an incredibly difficult time admitting that they are not prepared, especially in the first year. I cannot tell you how many times I bore witness to the slow moving train wreck of a fellow classmate stammering through an answer when they clearly had not done the reading. I was guilty of this behavior myself in the little anecdote above.

I am not sure whether 1Ls are afraid that they will look stupid in front of their classmates, or think that if they just dig deep enough they will come up with the answer. Whatever the reason, I promise you that you will save face by simply admitting that you are unprepared rather than trying to thread the needle. The professor may admonish you in front of the entire class for not reading—more likely they will glare at you for a few seconds before moving on—but it will be child's play compared to the reaming you will get after being exposed as a fraud. None of your classmates will judge you for being unprepared, and if they do, screw 'em—their number will get called soon enough.

Socratic Fire Drill

During the first few weeks, the prospect of being called on should be enough of an incentive for you to read the assigned cases and avoid going to class unprepared. For many of you, being prepared will breed confidence and you will charge into the classroom like a bat out of hell ready for whatever the professor throws your way.

However, as the class progresses and your name is not called, your initial burst of enthusiasm will diminish. This happens most frequently in classes where the professor conducts his questioning with only one or two students for an extended period of time, rather than jumping around rapid fire. With the professor moves quickly from student-to-student, you are forced to stay on your toes because at any time you might be next. But when the professor engages a single student in a long-drawn-out back and forth, which many professors will do, your attention span will be severely tested.

Unless you are a Luddite or your law school bans them, you are probably going to have your laptop with you in class. As your concentration deviates farther from the class discussion, the little white angel on your left shoulder will try hard to keep you focused and engaged. But the little red demon on your right shoulder is going to pressure you to give in and explore the plethora of fun and exciting information available at your fingertips on the World Wide Web.

If your red devil is as persuasive as mine was, he is going to win...a lot. Before you know it, you are surfing the information superhighway and have completely checked out of class. Let me say quickly that I am not encouraging you to explore the internet during class. But pretending that you aren't going to peruse the web is like preaching abstinence during Spring Break at the First Church of Cancun: *Just Say No* just doesn't work.

So there you are in class, checking scores on espn.com, catching-up on the latest gossip on perezhilton, or searching for attractive co-eds to stalk on Facebook, when suddenly, out of nowhere—*boom*...you hear your name called. Oh no...THIS... IS...NOT...HAPPENING.... You have absolutely no idea what case you are on, what the question was about, or even what class you are in....

Ok...let's get through this together: here are the steps for the *Socratic Fire Drill:*

First...take a deep breath. Don't panic. You have about a five-second window before the professor is going to call your name again. Use this time. Close down whatever you are looking at on the internet, open up your case notes for the class, and start to scroll through them. Check the time in the corner of your laptop. Depending on how far you are into the class, you can estimate how much of the material you have already covered. Scan down your notes to a section that approximately corresponds to where you *think* you are in the class.

At this point, the professor is going to call your name again, perhaps with a slightly more brusque inflection. Don't be intimidated. Methodically look up from your laptop and pretend that it is the first time that you heard him call your name. Make him think that you didn't respond the first time because you thought he was pronouncing your name wrong or his voice was muffled—not because you weren't paying attention. Sell it. Give him the, "Oh *me?*" look. Maybe bat your eyes a little [Gentleman: please consider whether batting your eyes is likely to be an effective tactic for you]…then, with just a hint of sugar:

"Professor Pissoff…would you mind repeating your question, please?"

It is important that you phrase it this way and not "can you say that again" (too curt), or "I'm not quite sure what the question is" (too ridiculous if the question was something simple such as "Can you please state the facts").

As soon as the word "please" leaves your tongue, immediately start looking through your notes and further narrow down where you think you are. As the professor repeats the question, you will have bought yourself enough time to listen to his query and simultaneously pinpoint your location. Because lead-off questions are often pretty general, you should be able to anchor yourself to the right case, offer a response, and proceed to speak with swagger and confidence. You have escaped the burning house without a scratch. Job well done.

We can learn a few lessons from the little scenario depicted above. For one, if you are a laptop user, *never* close your case notes or briefs; minimize them instead. That way you can pull them up quickly. It is an even better idea to keep them open at all times, minimize the viewing window, and position them next to whatever you are looking at on the internet. I would probably catch a lot of flack from professors and law school personnel for this advice, but I am not going to blow smoke up your arse and say that you are never going to surf the internet during class. If professors are going to insist on interrogating only a few students out of a large class for the entire class period, they should expect that some students will see fit to brush up on their recreational reading.

An important disclaimer: pulling off the Socratic Fire Drill is a tricky feat. When you are under the spotlight in a classroom with maybe 200 eyeballs on you, time moves very slo-o-w-w-w-l-y. If you doubt your ability to execute the Drill successfully, you can always default to Plan B and simply admit to the professor that you are lost. Chicken.

SORE THUMB

For those of you who get night tremors over the thought of being called on, a few pearls of wisdom might help you rest easier. I want to caution you that there is no way to completely dodge the Socratic bullet—*everyone* gets called on at some point. But the following bits of advice are invaluable for those who want to play it as close to the vest as possible.

First, I strongly advise against doing anything before or during class that draws attention to yourself or puts you on the professor's radar. I learned this lesson the hard way one semester when I went up to a professor after the first class to introduce myself and inform him that we had a mutual friend. We had a nice conversation and he was so appreciative that I made his acquaintance, he decided to thank me by calling on me at least three times as much anyone else. I would have preferred a pajama-gram.

Hence, if your goal is to avoid being called on as much as possible, try not to stick out like a sore thumb. Don't wear tacky Christmas sweaters during the holidays, dye your hair the color of a skittle, or beat box under your breath while you are listening to house music on cleverly concealed headphones. Yes, everyone will get called on eventually. But as you will soon see, professors will pick "favorites" and repeatedly call on the same people. Being inconspicuous is one of your better defenses.

MUSICAL CHAIRS

There seems to a common misconception among first years that choosing a seat in the back row is like wearing Socratic camouflage: The professor will never see you if you set up shop as far away from him or her as possible.

As it turns out, many law school professors have actually attended law school, and actually lived the strategies you're trying to employ. Thus, some have a back-row fetish and treat the blighted souls who sit there like stepchildren available for extra chores. I actually had a professor during first year who waged a personal vendetta against the back-row, to the point that it seemed he didn't know there *were* other rows in the classroom. Don't view the back-row as a panacea—that might be the first place a professor looks for prey.

Similarly, choosing a seat behind the more vertically endowed of your classmates can provide *temporary* cover for awhile. But eventually your plan will be revealed. I had one friend who thought that if he sat behind the tallest student in the class and slouched deep in his chair, the professor would never be able to find him. He called this operation "stealth mode" and likened it to flying low enough to avoid radar detection (he played lots of *Dungeons and Dragons* as a child, or maybe it was too much paste a few years before that). Soon enough, the professor's sonar tagged him and operation "stealth mode" was compromised. Feel free to try it, but realize it will only be temporary, because the professor does have an actual attendance roster and no matter how stealth you get, he will eventually get to your name.

THE PREEMPTIVE STRIKE

Much of the anxiety that comes from being called on stems from the worry that you are going to get a difficult question. Waiting to get called on means that you are at the mercy of the professor—whatever question he directs your way is the one that you are going to be forced to answer. Some students do not want to

relinquish this control and prefer to take matters into their own hands. Thus, the preemptive strike was born.

From time to time, professors will open questions up to the class and ask for volunteers. If the professor lobs a softball question or asks about something you know, it might not be a bad idea to raise your hand and volunteer. This puts the ball back in your court as opposed to leaving it entirely up to chance.

Of course, the professor can and often does stray from the initial question and go down a road you did not anticipate, but at least you will already be on the board. If the professor stays with you for a couple of minutes, your turn volunteering should be enough to take you off the hit list for a least one rotation of the class. Score one for the good guys.

TWEEDLE DFE AND TWEEDLE GUNNER

The previous sections were devoted to those among you who want to *avoid* speaking in class. What comes next is aimed at the individuals who revel in the spotlight and will enjoy participating.

Let me first state that being comfortable in front of your classmates is generally a good thing, and it will serve you well throughout law school and in your career. When you get into your second and third year, many professors will offer extra points for class participation and it can improve your grade, at least a little. Many of the best lawyers, especially litigators, are confident public speakers who have an impressive command over their audience. I can tell your first-hand that I learned a lot from classmates who offered insights and added value to class discussions. If you are a serial volunteer, however, you are going to toe a fine line between being a productive contributor to class discussion versus being what is commonly known as a "gunner."

Gunner is not a compliment.

Gunners are those who volunteer in class *all the time,* not because they want to contribute an interesting perspective or analysis, but rather because they love the sound of their own voice. I will tell you right now that no one will be impressed that you are a gunner, and you are going to be made fun of behind your back. I am not saying this to discourage the more loquacious and extroverted among you from participating; I'm just giving you the facts.

I am sure many famous legal scholars and influential jurists were gunners. I can picture a portly, twenty-something Antonin Scalia arriving to class 15 minutes early every day, chocolate Danish in tow, snagging a seat in the first row right, reflexively launching his hand into the air whenever the professor asked a question, giving a vociferous fist-pump every time he aced an answer, then devouring the Danish like it was the last thing he would eat before winter hibernation. If you aspire for this to be you—then feel free to skip what I am about to say.

If on the other hand, you want to know how to become an active contributor to class discussions without drifting into gunner territory—heed the following advice:

First, don't feel like you have to answer *every question* the professor asks. It's not just you two in the room. After you nail the first two or three in a row, your classmates will be impressed. After the next eight or nine, you will start to get on everyone's nerves; after the fifteenth or sixteenth, the rest of the class will want to string you up by your feet in the quad and use you as a human piñata. Spread the love a little bit and give others a chance. Pace yourself.

Second, if you do make the decision to be active in class, do not sit in the very front row. If you are severely near-sighted or have a stigmatism, then you get a pass—but if so, re-read the point about not jumping in *every* time. Otherwise, you should burn the following equation into your cerebral cortex: sitting in the front row + volunteering all the time = GUNNER. It's not that a big of a deal to choose another row, any row, just not the first.

Third, and this should be common sense, never disparage or disrespect another classmate by sighing, moaning, grunting, chuckling, or making any other unnatural, slightly disturbing noise while they are talking. People who engage in this type of behavior should have opted for charm school, not law school.

Being condescending is never cool. Al Gore lost a debate and probably the Presidency over this; you might lose friends if you do this. If you ever hope to socially interact with real people instead of FarmVille characters, extend your peers some courtesy and refrain from mocking them.

If you manage to do what I have suggested, you will be able to participate early and reasonably often without coming across as a pompous know-it all. Your classmates won't roll their eyes every time you raise your hand, or bash you on G-Chat while you wax poetic on the poor jurisprudential reasoning of Justice Marshall in *Marbury v. Madison.*

Don't be afraid to get involved and be an active participant in class discussions. But remember that trying desperately to prove that you are the smartest person in a class of other smart people will not earn you the respect of your classmates.

RESOLVE: IT'S MORE THAN JUST A STAIN REMOVER

Law professors love to make students second-guess themselves when discussing a case. You may give an answer that you are sure is correct only to find that the teacher challenges your reasoning and questions your thought process.

Don't get panicked—they are doing it on purpose. Professors are not going to ask black-and-white questions with clear answers that fit into neat little boxes. Instead, the questions are going to be difficult with a lot of grey area and room for disagreement. Your job is not necessarily to come up with the *right* answer; rather it is to *defend* your answer with a persuasive argument. If you feel confident about your answer, don't let the professor break your resolve by making you think that you are wrong. The tougher the questions get, the better you are probably doing.

After you get over the initial hump of speaking in class the first few times, it will become a lot less stressful for most of you. You will realize that no one is going to think you're stupid if you fumble over a question, and most people are not even listening that intently anyway.

Some, however, are *never* going to feel comfortable speaking in class, and to you I say...don't stress about it. Hardly any first-year professors include class participation in the final grade, and you will never be docked for getting a question wrong or being ineloquent (unless you repeatedly come to class unprepared, which I would not advise). Some of the best students in law school are not great public speakers and they still go on to successful and prosperous careers.

Very few times in your career are you going to be expected to speak about something that you do not know about in advance. Whether you are in trial or meeting with a partner at a firm, there is a good chance that you are going to know the topic that you will be discussing beforehand. In these situations, thinking on your feet is certainly important, but preparation is paramount. You will come to see that being well prepared can obviate many of your fears about public speaking.

As the wise prophet Yogi Berra once remarked, "I never said most of the things that I said." Praise be unto Yogi. Try not to beat yourself up if you have a bad showing in class. It will be a lot less of a big deal to others than it is to you, and within a day, it will be a distant memory. Just do the best you can and then *forget about it.* And if all else fails, picture the professor wearing nothing but cowboy boots, black leather chaps, and a spandex-leopard print one-piece.

Carrots from Uncle Malice:

- Accept that you are going to have at least one bad Socratic incident. Don't make it worse by making a scene.

- Don't try to B.S. your way through an answer when you are unprepared; your professor will know and can use the opportunity to make an example out of you.

- If the thought of speaking in class makes you break out in a cold sweat, do what you can to blend in and remain inconspicuous.

- Use preemptive strikes to put the ball back in your court and regain some control over the process.

- If you get called on when you are not paying attention, stay calm, follow the Socratic Fire Drill, and you will survive.

- Don't be an answer hog. Gunners never have weekend plans.

- At the end of the day, your relative ineloquence during a class discussion doesn't really matter. It will have no affect on your final grade, won't prevent you from being a successful attorney, and *no one will remember.* Relax, do your best, then forget about it.

VII

OUTLINING

*"What is the use of repeating all that stuff?" the Mock
Turtle interrupted, "if you don't explain it as you go on?"*

Starting around mid-October, it seemed that every day someone
was blathering about outlining. "Did you start outlining for
Torts yet?"; "Which outline are you going to use for Con Law?";
"Is the Professor going to give us an outline?"; "I'll show you my
outline if you show me yours!"; "Does this outline make me look
fat?" I would nod and smile like I knew what these people were
talking about even though I really didn't. Well, allow me to
unravel this spellbinding mystery for you right now so you don't
experience the same confusion.

An outline is a chronological compilation of all the case
briefs and notes that you prepare throughout the semester condensed into one giant study guide that you will use to study for
finals. *Outlining* is the process of preparing the outline using all
of your notes and briefs. But outlining is not *just* a compilation
of your notes and briefs—after all, what if your notes suck and
briefs dropped off after the first week?

An outline is also a *distillation* of the entire law of that subject, using everything you were supposed to study, and more:
case law (briefs), class discussion (notes), and everything else—
including stuff that was never covered in class. Now you know
why exams are so fun.

Note: while outlines are a distillation of the "entire" law on
that subject, it's not literally true that you need to know everything. What you *do* need to know are *all* of the *basic* points that
were covered in class or should have been covered in class or
were poorly covered in class or that were mangled by bad

Socratic dialogue. Essentially, your outline should be a survey of the major points of that subject.

When you sit down to begin the task of studying for your first set of finals, you will be overwhelmed by the sheer amount of notes and information that you have to review. This is where outlining becomes an effective way to study. Starting with the first cases that you read and proceeding through the semester, you will construct an outline of the holdings from each case that will, in the aggregate, be the body of law that you will need to know for that particular subject. Now you see why I suggested writing the **issue** and **holding** in big bold letters under every case name; this will save you valuable time because you won't have to re-read long briefs in order to remember these important takeaways. Sometimes people include a synopsis of the reasoning or rationale in their outline because it helps them understand why the court came out a certain way and further elucidates the legal reasoning behind the decision.

As you soon realize, there is a wide assortment of commercial outlines available for you to buy that cover every subject that you will study during the first year. Because many of these outlines are comprehensive, lots of law students purchase and use them instead of writing their own. If you are one of the few who can retain information just by reading it, then spending hours composing a long outline is probably not the most effective use of your time and you should look into buying great commercial outlines. Commercial outlines come in many different formats, so go to your campus bookstore and thumb through several styles to see which best suits you.

I did not like using commercial outlines because I need to write stuff down in my own words to really learn it. Accordingly, the process of reviewing my briefs and composing my own outline was the best way for me to study. I did buy commercial outlines to help supplement my studying because they helped me make sense of difficult or confusing legal doctrines. I recommend that you do the same even if you plan on making your own outlines. As you begin the process of studying, you will figure out which strategy works best for you and proceed from there.

One last word about outlines and then we can move on. In every class, there is a group of students who will get *very* competitive about their outlines. I am not sure why exactly this happens, but my theory is that this misplaced competitive spirit derives from a famous scene in the movie *The Paper Chase,* which undoubtedly a relative has purchased for you by now, in which a small study group of 1Ls at Harvard Law School fight over who has the best outline.

In the magical world of cinema, this makes for an amusing scene. In real life, you will sound like a complete putz if you start boasting about your outline or your outlining *skillz.* Accordingly, the following phrases should never leave your mouth: "My outline is one sexy beast—bet you wish you could touch it;" "My outline is ridic (please don't ever say "ridic" in any context); "If my outline were a person, I would definitely have sex with it;" And the old classic., "My outline is on fire...don't stand too close because you might get burned...*sssssss!*"

You are going to be surprised by the stupid things people say in law school. And they are going to say them with such bravado that you will unconsciously find yourself cocking your head like a confused dog and wondering if they are actually serious. Sadly, many of them are. Try to remember that your outline is a law school study aid, not a leggy Scandinavian model or a Maserati.

Carrots from Uncle Malice:

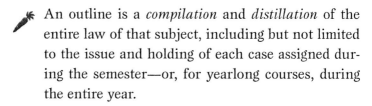 An outline is a *compilation* and *distillation* of the entire law of that subject, including but not limited to the issue and holding of each case assigned during the semester—or, for yearlong courses, during the entire year.

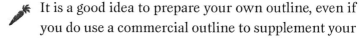 It is a good idea to prepare your own outline, even if you do use a commercial outline to supplement your

work and to help you make sense of difficult points of law.

Bragging about your outline: as cool as socks with sandals. Just a tip.

VIII

FINALS

"That's the most important piece of evidence we've heard yet," said the King, rubbing his hands; "...so now let the jury—"

"If any one of them can explain it," said Alice "I'll give him sixpence. I don't believe there's an atom of meaning in it."

In an alternate law school utopia, at the end of the semester, every law school would throw a lavish cocktail party complete with top-shelf open bar, nude ice sculptures of the nine Supreme Court Justices (maybe not Scalia), and an all-you-can eat lobster buffet (replete with portabella burgers for the vegans and *Hebrew National* dogs for you kosher kids). Gunners would be tasked with de-shelling the crustaceans tableside. Professors would be responsible for keeping each student's individual fondue pot of drawn butter at just the right temperature.

If at any point during the meal, your butter got too hot, or too cold, you would have permission to order the derelict butter attendant, let's call him Professor Butter-Fail, to promptly march to the front of the resplendent dining hall. There, in front of the entire party, you would have the opportunity to question Professor Butter-Fail about the correct boiling point of fermented cream (in metric units of course). Perhaps your lead off question would go something like, "Professor Butter-Fail, could you please recite for the party, in correct chronological order, how cream is turned into butter...and I think that everyone in the dining hall would appreciate if you didn't read directly from your notes...."

At the end of the feast, every student would receive a glowing report card to tack on the refrigerator commending them on their great work during the semester. Instead of letter grades, this report card would simply contain a giant smiley (J) next to every subject; if your (J) was winking at you, that would of course indicate superlative work.

And as tacit acknowledgement of appreciation for your extortion, *er...* tuition dollars, the admissions office would put together an elaborate gift basket for you to enjoy over winter break stocked full of the best swag (*i.e.* glow-in-the-dark condoms; a digital version of the Kama Sutra; a $100 gift certificate to In & Out Burger; a year's supply of watermelon Big-League chew; and a chinchilla comforter to keep you warm during those cold winter months). No tests, no stress, just a good time and some cool party favors.

For some reason, law schools have not shared my vision, and opt instead to end the semester with a somewhat different rite of passage—final exams. Hands down, nothing causes more stress for first-year students than finals.

I won't lie to you, it is not the most fun thing that you will do in your life. But as with everything else in law school, the more you know about it from the beginning, the less scary it is when it actually happens. With that in mind, I will try to demystify some of the myths and mysteries surrounding finals and prepare you for what to expect and how to best approach it.

Let me remind you that in *no way* do you need to be worrying about finals yet, unless it is December and you just purchased this book, along with your textbooks for the semester (in which case I would like to thank you for your purchase and wish and you and your family a happy holiday season). But if you read this now and then review it again come finals time, it may help take some of the edge off. Think of this section as finals Xanax.

Finals are stressful for two reasons. The first reason is obvious—many students believe that grades are a matter of life and death. Most likely, your grade on the final exam *will* constitute your entire grade for that course. Your final exam at the end of a year-long course will probably be the entire grade for that subject. And, yes, law firms are extremely sensitive to grades, especially in a bad job market. Thus, the thinking goes, the better that you do on your finals, the higher that you will rank in your class, the better job you will get, the more money you will make out of law school, and the cooler you will be.

While it is true that home-run grades can lead to more lucrative job opportunities *initially,* that does not mean that the most successful attorneys all graduated at the top of their class. And I know for a fact that many of the people who *did* graduate at the top of their class are the same people that you would *least* want to sit next to on a transatlantic flight (also on that list: Dominique Strauss-Kahn; Snooki; and Courtney Love).

I am not suggesting that you throw in the towel early and not give finals the old college try. I know that many of you are serious overachievers who have never received a grade lower than a 97 in your life. But you should try to maintain a modicum of perspective on the relative importance that law school finals will have on your life. It will be a hell of a lot less of a big deal that it seems when you are going through it. Your success as a lawyer, or in another career, is not going to depend on your grade on your Torts final.

There is another reason that finals stress people out. For almost an entire semester, you have been working hard, reading cases and trying to master complex material. Yet, other than the occasional jousting with your professor, you probably have not been tested in any way that actually quantifies your progress and empirically tests your knowledge. You may feel that you have no idea whether you are actually learning anything or whether this supposedly valuable law school education is worth the hefty price of admission. I know that is how I felt.

Then here comes finals, a whole semester's worth of hard work is boiled down to one test to determine whether you actually "get it." Personally, I think it is incredibly unfair to reduce an entire semester to one test because there are a variety of reasons that students might not do well on exams even though they have worked hard during the semester and understand the material.

You may have read every Civil Procedure case backwards and forwards, but the day that your final rolls around, you come down with a bad flu and a throbbing headache that make it impossible for you to concentrate. Maybe you are having personal problems and taking a law school exam is the last thing on your mind. And some people simply are not great test takers: they comprehend the subject matter when they read it but just cannot manage to apply it on a timed exam. These are all valid reasons why using a single exam to distill a semester's worth of hard work into a one grade is inherently misguided.

Nonetheless, that is how law school curricula have been designed since the olden days and it probably will continue into the distant future. But don't think, because your final grade is not as high as you wanted, that you have wasted valuable time and energy. If you do all the work to the best of your ability and truly grapple with the material, you should feel a sense of accomplishment, regardless of how you do on the exam. And despite what you think, I guarantee that you have learned more than you realize. Okay, enough with the *Lifetime* Movie of the Week monologue—time to get down to brass tacks.

JUST THE FACTS, MA'AM…OH, AND THE REASONS TOO

At almost every law school in the country, you will be given a final exam at the end of the semester for each major class. Although there is no uniform format common to all law schools, the overwhelming majority of exams consist of a set of hypothetical facts involving fictitious parties. Some exams may consist of one long set of facts, while others will have multiple questions comprised of distinct facts for each question. The facts given on the exam are referred to as the "fact pattern."

Perhaps in an effort to add a bit of levity to an otherwise tense situation, law school professors will construct fact patterns that involve celebrities or famous people who get involved in precarious or embarrassing situations. I promise you that the humor is lost in the heat of the exam. Plus, like a lot of the professors who write them, most aren't funny anyway.

After you read the fact pattern, you will be expected to apply the law from the respective class to the facts given and answer a

question or series of questions. Sometimes the question may be general such as "Assess John's claims under Contract Law," or more specific, such as, "Are there any defenses to John's claim that the contract is invalid?"

You will often hear law professors say that they are less concerned with the actual answer that you give and more focused on the reasoning behind your answer. They mean it. Referring to the second example question given above, even if you answer, "No—there are no defenses to John's claim that the Contract is invalid." when really there are defenses, you can still earn points by clearly explaining your reasoning *why* there are no defenses. If your reasoning makes sense to the Professor, you will score some points (more on "scoring" below).

Every answer to *every question* should be supported with *reasoning.* Never assume that the professor will understand what you mean or that you get it. You need to spell it out. Think out loud on exams by explaining your thought process—every detail.

TIME!

For most, the time element is the most difficult aspect of the exam. Without time constraints, many students could probably reason their way through the questions and eventually come up with good answers. It is a different story when you are limited to three or four hours. This might seem quite generous. It is not. Remember that you need to explain your reasoning for every step along the way, and at the same time draw a concise, logical path. This *is* hard. Stay cognizant of the time remaining as you work through each part of the exam—don't get bogged down if you don't know the answer to a certain question.

Similarly, don't answer one question with a lengthy dissertation covering every possible angle while ignoring another question entirely. What you gain in points on the good answer you will lose, big time, on the question that you don't answer. Think about it this way: you might get an extra half-point here and there for insightful comments on tertiary issues, but you will lose *all* of the points, major and minor, for what you don't answer at all.

Professors often specify how many points each question is worth; pay attention to the point apportionment and make sure that you devote the appropriate time to the more heavily weighted questions.

Count It!

The goal of law exams is to get as many points as possible. The way you get points is by applying the correct law with substantive analysis to the appropriate facts given. Thus, you will frequently hear about *issue spotting.*

On most exams, professors are going to bury many legal issues within the hypothetical facts. Some of these issues will be obvious and some of them will be harder to uncover. It will be your job to identify as many of these legal issues as possible, apply the correct law thereto, and support your application of the law with thoughtful reasoning.

Which brings me to an important point—if they provide them, *look at past exams given by your professors.* My first exam in law school was a four-hour, closed-book property law exam. Property is one of the more difficult classes first year and I studied like crazy for the test, but still did not feel confident about the material. Two days before the exam, one of my friends asked me if I had reviewed the professor's past exams that he had posted online. Until that moment, I had no clue that the professor had posted past exams and was thankful that my friend clued me in. I studied the past exams posted online and felt slightly more comfortable having familiarized myself with the professor's style of testing.

On exam day, I will never forget the moment that I opened the first page of the property exam only to find an exact replica of one of the exams that the professor had posted online. Every word of every question was exactly the same.

After I got over the initial shock of what had happened, and realized this was really going down, I began churning out answers that I had already seen before. Now, what the professor did for my property final was not kosher and he had hell to pay with the furious students who had failed to review the past exams. It was not right of the professor to do this given that so many students had spent so much time studying the material. And I certainly would not count on this same thing happening to you. I only share this anecdote to emphasize that importance of looking at past exams. It will help familiarize you with the professor's style of testing and bring to light to your professor's particular formatting preferences. Never assume that future exams will be a mirror image of past ones; but often they will provide clues. Check them out.

OPEN SESAME

Many law exams will be open book, or modified open book, which essentially means that the professor will allow you to bring notes, outlines, or other specified references into the exam with you. In contrast, closed book is just what it sounds like— you all by your lonesome with nothing but a pen and a laptop.

On balance, most students prefer the open book exams because there is the added comfort of knowing that you can look at your notes. I strongly caution you not to view open-book exams as a free-pass to avoid studying. Yes, you will have essentially all the information that you need right in front of you. But a semester's worth of work is a lot of material and no matter how organized you are, relying too heavily on notes will create real problems.

The time constraint of the exam makes it crucial that you answer questions quickly. If you are spending time frantically rummaging through your notes on an open-book exam, you will not do well. Your sneaky professors will construct exams in such a way that the open-book component will not be much help, and may actually be a hindrance. Finally, remember that everyone else has the same open-book "benefit."

If there are certain concepts that you are having an especially difficult time with, organize them clearly in your outline so that you can locate them *quickly* when you are taking the exam. For this reason, you should actually build two outlines: a full outline with all of the detail you have digested, and a condensed outline with only the most important details (which you can be almost certain will be tested).

So, for example, court opinions with multi-pronged legal tests are ripe for the condensed outline. (Say what?? Don't worry—after the first week of class you will know what a "multi-prong" legal test is—can you tolerate the suspense?) This type of material can be difficult to memorize and should be readily accessible during the test. On an open-book exam, think of your notes as bumpers on a bowling lane-they are there to put you back on track if you need them but *the goal should be to come into contact with them as infrequently as possible, if ever.*

LATHER, RINSE, STUDY, REPEAT

How you study for finals is largely a personal decision—but that doesn't mean anything goes.

First, do not wait until the last minute to start. "Last minute" means "within one month of exams." Re-read that as necessary: one *month* before exams. Law exams are different from undergraduate exams; cramming will not work. Re-read that as well: cramming will not work. What you saw in *The Paper Chase,* where the hero blocks himself in a hotel room to study 24/7 before exams, is merely a side room down the rabbit hole. There is simply too much material for you to put off studying until the last minute.

For some law students, chronic procrastination is not a problem because they are anxious about finals and start studying early in the semester. Some will advise you that over-studying too early in the semester will cause you to burn out. This is true, but only if you are doing it wrong. "Doing it wrong" means anything that does not help you apply your knowledge of black letter law to a fact pattern—*i.e.,* a final exam. So, rearranging type-face colors in your notes is doing it wrong. Re-color-coding your casebooks is doing it wrong.

A better way to study is simply to stay current with your out-line, which requires that you stay current with your readings and briefs and actively identify the legal issues and holdings from each case. At the end of the case, you should know why that case was there—why it was assigned to you—and you should be able to state the holding as a simple rule. Master the concepts as you learn them.

Don't worry about how much other people are studying. Anyone who claims to have studied for fourteen hours a day for sixteen weeks straight is either: (1) an avatar who subsists sole-ly on honeysuckle and cactus water; (2) tying to mess with you [in which case you need to walk away; seriously…walk. away]; or (3) full of shit.

Everyone has a different threshold for how much informa-tion they can process at one time. You will find yours. Just don't fall into the trap of thinking that you can waltz into the exam room after having done a 72-hour "study" marathon and feel pre-pared. Try this: two months before finals, download Nick Nolte's mug shot, with the Hawaiian shirt and electro-shock hairdo, for your computer background. Look at it every day as a reminder of what you will feel like if you attempt a three-day cram session.

GROUP THINK

First-year law students love to form *study groups.* Sometimes, they love to *think* about forming study groups. Or, once they have a study group, to pretend to actually study in their "study" group.

You are going to have to decide whether this is the right move for you. Study groups are small groups of students who meet to discuss the material and study together. Sometimes groups decide to study only during finals, or just before finals. This is dangerous for reasons mentioned above. If you're only coming to terms with the legal concepts just before finals, you are way behind. And if your study group is only getting its act together in the last month, chances are good that the time you spend together will be more distracting than it is helpful. This is because someone in your group will be confused about a particular concept, or multiple concepts. But rather than confidently resolving this individual's questions, the confusion will spread through the group like wildfire. It is unsettling when you think that you understand the material and someone says, "Wait! I thought this doctrine meant the exact opposite." Now you're going to waste time trying to figure out who is right. And even if you do get it figured out, you have increased the likelihood that will get confused during the exam because in the heat of a test, it is easy to jumble up concepts that were just recently (re)learned.

Sometimes groups will meet during the semester and actually get real learning done. Often, however, these "study sessions" are smoke and mirrors. They are less about studying than they are about socializing and blowing off steam. For example, many study groups will decide to "share" outlines. This seems logical. They'll divvy up the courses and make each person responsible for a specific subject. The group will supposedly hash out a single outline, which should theoretically cut down on the time that each person would have spent individually compiling the entire outline by himself. But as you might guess, this doesn't always work as it is supposed to. Often someone completely flakes on the group, leaving everyone stranded—especially if it is later in the semester. Sometimes someone doesn't flake, but they do a poor job with their assigned subject. Or maybe they do complete their work, but they are wrong on key issues or omit important material.

Almost always everyone gets so busy that they stop cross-checking other peoples' work and simply accept what they say. This has three dangers: (1) something could be wrong; (2) something could be missing; and (3) even if nothing is wrong or missing and it's the most perfect outline in the history of outlines, preparing for law exams requires more than simply *reading* another individual's interpretation of the law. You have to *know* it.

I hated study groups for a few reasons. Primarily, 1Ls are prone to freaking out about exams and correspondingly they will severely over-study. When I say over-study, I mean that students will get bogged down in the minutiae of cases and spend hours focusing on details that you will never be asked on the exam. If you have the misfortune of belonging to a study group with some of these individuals, their over-zealous approach may make you feel like your efforts have been inadequate. This, of course, means that you need to know what is "minutiae," and what is genuinely important. Here's Uncle Malice to tell you: if it's a rule that is part of black letter law discussed in class or a major heading in a commercial outline, it's genuinely important. If it's the number of stripes in Chief Justice Rehnquist's robe, that's minutiae.

I remember going to my first study group feeling that I knew the material pretty well, only to be completely emasculated by a woman who could spout off the name of every plaintiff from every case that we had read in the class. It was impressive, true, but *it was also a complete waste of her time.* Knowing a plaintiff's name is absolutely irrelevant: it would never score her any points on an exam. But, her intensity seriously scared me. I decided that everyone in the group knew more than I did, and I promptly defected.

The other reason I never liked study groups is because I generally felt that I had a pretty good grasp of what material I needed to work on and what I already understood. Thus, it was not an effective use of my time to re-review material that I was already comfortable with just so someone else in my group could learn it. Conversely, I did not want to breeze over the material that I did not know because everyone in the group already understood it.

For these reasons, I found it more helpful to study alone. But just because this worked for me does not me that it will be the right approach for you. Many of the concepts that you will come across during the first year are difficult to understand, and no matter how many times you study them by yourself, you may not know if you truly get it. In these instances, it will help you to discuss the concepts with other people. Or, if you're simply more social, you might enjoy talking through the concepts with others.

Talking through difficult material can be an invaluable exercise because it will give you a better idea of what you know. The ability to articulate legal concepts out loud and explain them in plain English is a sign that you get it. And a good study partner can help you make sense of a difficult issue that is giving you problems. Keep an open mind about study groups, maybe attend a meeting or two, and you will be able to decide whether they make sense for you.

One more thing: the point of study groups is not to "study," but to prepare for exams. So, if what you're doing in your group is not helping you immediately and directly in applying what you know to a bizarre fact pattern, you should think about whether a study group is the best use of your time.

THE NUTHOUSE

Law school libraries are quiet enclaves filled with hushed students diligently working to finish their homework before class or the weekend. I found it easier to get work done in the library, because it did not tempt me with the same forbidden fruits available elsewhere.

During finals, however, this otherwise placid academic arena is transformed into an unchecked insane asylum populated by feral wildebeests strung out on bad coffee and prescription uppers. The stress and fear emanating from your panicked classmates will seep into your pores and you too will start to feel like a prisoner in Shawshank.

Needless to say, I avoided the library at all cost during finals. I found it difficult to keep my chi aligned in a room populated by raving lunatics who would gladly sacrifice their first-born for a better outline. If you are eager to be part of this depraved circus, then go right ahead and set up shop in your school's library. But don't say that you weren't warned.

For those who not wish to participate in a live reenactment of *One Flew over the Cuckoo's Nest,* coffee shops and public libraries away from the law school can provide a quiet and peaceful sanctuary to study. Or, if you have yogi-like concentration, stay in your flannel and slippers and never leave the friendly confines of your apartment or home. Try a few places earlier in the semester and see where you feel the most comfortable and focused.

If you can, you should make a serious effort to exercise. Go for a walk or at least get out of your apartment for a few hours every day to get some air. It used to annoy me when professors would suggest this because it seemed trite—but they are right. Taking breaks and interacting with other humans (especially non-1L humans) will provide a nice respite from the monotony of studying that will be your life for several months, and it will make it slightly more tolerable.

GAME DAY

When the day of your first final actually rolls around, there are a few important dos and don'ts to remember.

If you are taking a morning final, do not skip breakfast. Do not take the test on an empty stomach, or eat anything that's weird. Most finals are three hours long and you need some fuel running through your veins to stay sharp. Stay away from triple espressos, pixie sticks, and any other snack or beverage that will give you a serious buzz and then cause you to crash. A heavy dose of fiber, although an important staple of any balanced diet, is probably not a wise choice either.

Plan on getting to the exam early. Make sure your computer and program are set up and running. (Your school will have a software program for you to use to take the final; be sure you're not learning about this the morning of the exam.) Give yourself an extra window of time to make sure the program is running, especially on your first set of exams. You're already going to be stressed. A computer glitch of any kind on exam day is going to take you to the breaking point—maybe beyond. This is preventable if you simply make sure that everything is working in advance. In fact, you might even have a spare laptop and make sure that is ready too.

Another reason to get to school early is to ensure that you nab a good seat where you will be comfortable, or at least not uncomfortable. These tests are three hours, sometimes more. Be sure you're going to last. Grandma Malice used to remind me to always wear layers: the woman's wisdom knows no bounds, and you should listen to her like I did.

I had a certain seat that I liked to sit in (very back row, second from the left), so I would get to school *way* ahead of time to stake my claim. I was also particular about how my personal space was arranged; I liked my writing materials on the right side and my meds on the left. If you are picky about these sorts of things, as I was, it is a good idea to be on the early side so you can secure the right seat and properly feng-shui your area before the test.

That's finals in a nutshell. I alluded to this early in the chapter but I think it is worth repeating: strive to keep this in perspective. Finals are stressful, and yes they are important...but you *will* get through it. Don't let your classmates freak you out, and don't think that your future success as a lawyer depends on your first semester grades. Get yourself organized, study hard, and then party like a wild banshee when the last one is over.

Carrots from Uncle Malice:

- Look at professors' old exams. The ones posted by your professors are the most helpful. But check other professors' exams as well. Old exams are one of your best study tools.

- "Study" does not mean memorize. It means "be able to draw, at a rapid pace, upon a deep knowledge of the legal rules to write a persuasive, precise answer to a bizarre fact pattern."

Study in the library at your own peril.

Be opened-minded about study groups; they can be helpful, but only under certain circumstances. Be sure those circumstances are right for you.

On exam day, arrive early

Medicate any post-finals depression with Drs. Jim, Jack, and Crown. But always medicate responsibly.

IX

GRADES

"If everybody minded their own business, the world would go around a great deal faster than it does."

Four to six weeks after your last final, you will receive a notification of some kind informing you that your professors have started to post grades. Your first set of law school grades is unquestionably the most nerve-racking, made worse by the constant talk about on-campus interviews, the job market, and everything related to what those grades will mean. You will also be seeking some validation for all of the work and energy expended during the past semester. This stamp of approval (or disapproval) comes in the form of a half-dozen letters, most centered around the second letter in our alphabet.

I am not going to give you the pre-packaged speech about not letting yourself get too wrapped up in grades or thinking that they mean everything; you shouldn't and they don't. But it will seem that way. Ultimately, you are going to have to decide this for yourself. It always seemed disingenuous when I heard the same message from my professors. I found it paradoxical that professors bombard you with work, stress you out about the exam, and then tell you not to take your grades too seriously.

For many students, grades are very important and they *will* define their success in law school by their G.P.A. Individuals with aspirations to work at silk-stocking firms are going to place a *lot* of emphasis on their grades. This is just the reality of the first year.

I am going to offer only one piece of advice about grades: no matter how awesome or poorly that you do, *don't discuss* your grades with other people. This is a losing proposition for everyone. If you did fantastic and ask your friends and classmates how they did because you want them to ask you back, you are going to come off like a pompous ass. Nothing is more annoying than a 1L who wants everyone to know how well he or she did on exams.

On the other hand, if you did not do great, it will be tempting to ask other people about their grades in hopes of finding solidarity with a friend who didn't do well either. But I promise that you are going to end up feeling worse when you find out that they did better than you.

Whichever end of the spectrum you fall on, or anywhere in between, do not put others in the position of having them tell you their grades. It is personal, and it is really no one's business but your own. Don't ask. Don't tell.

Did I say that I was only going to offer one piece of advice about finals and wasn't going to give you a pre-packaged speech about not getting too wrapped up? I lied. I have one more little pearl for you. If you don't do as well on finals as you would have liked, and you feel like you are going to "die," or that your "life is over," go find a newspaper and scan the major headlines to see what is happening around the world. Now tell me which one doesn't belong: War. Famine. Poverty. Injustice. Susie got a "B" in Civ Pro.

I know it feels shitty to get a bad grade after your worked your ass off. And I understand that your career aspirations are going to flash before your eyes. But those feelings will be fleeting. When you are feeling your worst, take a step back and think about how many people would kill to be in your shoes and even have the opportunity to sit for a law school exam. Your best weapon against grade hysteria is perspective: invite her into your life and an "82" in Con Law won't seem like the end of the world.

Carrots from Uncle Malice

 Grades are like pregnancy tests: advertising the results is totally uncouth. Keep it between you and your loved ones—and even then it can be good to wait a while.

X

ODDS AND ENDS

"No, no!" said the Queen. "Sentence first—verdict afterwards."

I want to mention a few important things that we did not discuss because I don't think that it is vital for you to be concerned with them yet. I only bring them up so that you are aware of their existence.

You will spend mountains of time in your first year with legal-writing projects: memos and persuasive briefs. These are part of your first year Legal Research & Writing/Legal Practice classes and are very different from what you will do in your other classes. Depending on the law school, Legal Research & Writing/Legal Practice may go by different names. But both classes will be focused on the same set of skills: teaching you the basic elements of the legal-research and legal-writing processes.

Legal writing is unlike any writing that you have done before. It is completely different from the writing you did in college, and it is not at all like the work that you'll be doing for your core subjects. Be patient when you first start and know that there is a steep learning curve. Most legal writing professors and TAs make themselves available to students. Don't hesitate to meet with them. Work through your difficulties with them—and work through those difficulties early. Don't wait until everyone is panicking; they'll be a lot less available to you then.

For some inexplicable reason, many law schools still make your learn legal research in the library using actual *print copies* of the resources. This is like teaching people how to use a Walkman instead of an iPod. But then again, "modern" is not a word generally associated with law schools.

In the real world, almost all the legal research that you will ever do will be conducted on one of two electronic databases: Westlaw and LexisNexis. Drop either one of those terms next time you are at a bar if you are looking to have to a quiet drink alone. Legal Research is not the most exciting class, but getting good at research will make your life easier when you begin writing your memos and persuasive briefs as an actual attorney.

Beyond these additional subjects, there are a host of other programs, clubs, activities, and groups. Ask questions, seek out events and programs of interest, stay active, and you will figure it all out.

XI

Peeking Behind the Curtain

"It was a curious dream, dear, certainly; but now run in to your tea: it's getting late."

Well, my friends, our trip has come to an end. You should no longer feel like you are going down the rabbit hole, alone, without anyone to guide you. Uncle Malice will be with you for the whole ride. But before we part ways, your Uncle Mal needs to say one more thing: there is a 500-pound Gorilla in our midst and we need to talk about it.

The choice to attend law school is harder than it has been in recent memory. The economic crisis battered law firms and caused many to drastically reduce their hiring. Consequently, there are fewer legal jobs than law graduates, and there is no way to know when, or if, the market will get better. The idea of taking on high levels of debt and committing three years of your life to prepare for a job that may not be waiting for you after graduation is scary. It is natural to question your decision and to worry about what the future may (or may not) hold.

I would be lying if I told you that I know everything is going to get better and that you should no have problem landing a great job after you graduate. We have just traveled 90 pages together through a bullshit-free zone and I am not going to start heaping it on now. Shallow anecdotes about how nice it will be for you to know how to read a lease or form an LLC aren't much consolation when you have student-loan payments to make and a family to support. But what I can do is offer a few thoughts based on my personal experience. Take them or leave them.

I graduated from law school in May of 2009, right in the eye of the economic storm. Before the market imploded, I clerked two summers at a large corporate firm in the Midwest. They offered me a position, which I accepted. I practiced corporate and securities law for a grand total of ten and one-half months before I decided to leave the law and pursue other interests.

When people hear my tale, they often ask me if I regret "wasting" three years of my life in law school. Allow me to tell you what I tell them: not for one second. In my opinion, law school is not about memorizing the elements of assault and battery or learning the difference between tenants in common and tenants by the entirety. To derive real value from your law degree, I don't even think that you need to ever practice law.

What I came to realize, and what has ultimately been the most enduring piece of my legal education, is captured by the following maxim: there are always at least two sides to every story. Studying the law involves studying opposing arguments. Some arguments may seem misguided, unsubstantiated, cruel, or even downright evil. But, whether you are preparing a legal brief, contemplating opening a business, or fighting with a loved one, your capacity to act prudently, and compassionately, is immeasurably improved by your willingness to thoughtfully consider the other side(s) of the story. Too few of our politicians, business leaders, friends, and family remember to practice this discipline.

I recognize that my take-away won't help you land that white-shoe associate gig or nail-down a prestigious clerkship. However, many of you aren't going to end up being lawyers and some of you may never step foot in a law firm. But, whatever path you choose, personally and professionally, it is *guaranteed* to involve conflict. And at the root of every conflict will be an opposing viewpoint; someone who sees things differently than you do. If you can draw upon your legal training in order to put yourself in the other person's shoes and force yourself to try to understand what they are thinking, you will make better decisions, solve more problems, and advance past those who are unwilling to open their minds. The daunting conflicts that you will inevitably face become more surmountable when you see the world through a *looking glass* other than your own.

Royal After Word

This is your King.

As a good and patient Sovereign, I shall strive with forbearance and quietude to understand my subjects, including most immediately those seeking service in entrance into the guilds of law.

I shall thus endeavor to humour the many misconceptions and, more troubling, the growing impertinence of our younger subjects as brought to me from all corners of the kingdom. In this royal communiqué, I shall abstain from delicate judgments but I am nonetheless duty-bound to mark my royal words as the final authority in the law and in the study thereof.

It has come to my attention that there is disquiet in the realm of law, and in particular in the halls of our petit schools of jurisprudence. Of direct concern comes a missive from Thaddeus Hatter, an amiable and peaceable if somewhat spirited subject.

* * *

Mr. Hatter offers a ready autopsy of a common approach to law school among many who enter: to go in with "as little information as humanly possible."

Mr. Hatter goes on to explain that, "[a]fter several months in a cloud of stress and bewilderment," he had "gradually emerged from the ether and started to make sense of the vexing mysteries of law school."

Hmm.

As you may know I too walked this path many years ago, and while I did so with royal infallibility, I was not blind to the sufferings around me. I am thus compelled to share a conviction: that many law students never do figure out law school, or the law. They just get by. And in this sea of subsistence-mediocrity, survival somehow seems enough. What's worse, what these hapless apprentice-subjects think they know is, in the main, wrong.

In my kingdom, this is unacceptable.

Law students focus on formulaic case briefs, without in any genuine sense understanding their true importance; or pro forma outlines, without understanding *their* importance; or boisterous or cantankerous class participation, without ever truly internalizing how and why it is so *un*important, in the way most assume it is vital.

Law students scribble notes as if building replicas of the great Cliffs of Dover, sheet by sheet, and never wonder why in the end it all seems so useless. Yet come spring, what do they do but revert to type. Literally. One can see law students pounding away at their infernal machines, as if half possessed of the feigned passions of kindergarten through college, hopeful that these shall make a difference when their law exam is passed before them—an exam testing the real application of my laws.

Law students never realize that those "hypos" they've been hearing about—and to a disappointingly great degree ignoring—are the meat of the law, because the fact that a fact pattern is true or made up is irrelevant to what law school (and the law) are all about: legal analysis. A barrister at an Inn of Court thinks through a fact pattern in essentially the same way whether in a law office or conference room or fancy restaurant or on an exam.

Law students in our kingdom focus, unacceptably, on the trivial and useless, and ignore the crucial and helpful.

This will not do.

Law students wonder why it is all so impenetrable and ominous, and then screech to the gods at the injustices of it all. What's worse, and amusing in a way of the Dark Arts, is the psychological force with which supposedly bright apprentice-subjects cling to their peevish and palpably injudicious beliefs. As if such fervent fidelity will serve as protection, they lash out at other subjects, loyal and true, who point out the obvious. The world is not flat. And I, as King, will stand not for such foolishness or impudence.

They respond with patently absurd fallacies, and are vicious in silencing dissenters. Academic freedom, indeed. They are snarky, or so I am told. A rapier wit is always in style—but only with a purpose and with a sense of ultimate humility. Such seems lacking in the kingdom of late. What is unacceptable is the closing of minds—which I and my regal predecessors have seen fit to free—and to force forward petty truths and the irrelevant and sometimes harmful common "wisdoms" set against the grander timeless truths of life and our society.

The sun, we now know, does not revolve around the Earth. What most young students think is "study" is not, and what even second- and third-year law apprentices think is correct and proper are also often not; they're all too caught up in their own bizarre Wonderlands to realize just how upside down this world really is.

My commands are thus:

Accept no wisdom from a peer without skeptical critique.

Reject no advice from a peer-elder without skeptical self-critique.

Offer no wisdom without humbling humility.

Read widely, and adopt patterns of study that are both time-lessly wise and sufficient for your own purposes—but not because they are seductive to a laziness of mind.

* * *

My royal advisors suggested a more specific set of royal guidance. To provide such, I shall narrow the commands further:

Brief a handful of cases early in your official studies, if not before. Do so fully. Spend two hours per case; no more, no less. Become familiar with the layout and with every fact and nuance. Then continue to do so until you understand why this is a distraction.

Use these cases to crystallize your own thinking about that area of the law, and do so with unreserved energy.

Focus not on procedural history or such other piddling details; while important to my clerks of court, they are mere trifles in the greater majesty of understanding the law of the land.

Waste not your time attempting to memorize obscure cases for, say, my law of Torts—which has a thousand of them. But take note where something remarkable is going on, such as when there's a "split of opinion" (a major rift in how my courts handle a certain issue), or perhaps certain of my juridical experts rule in a particularly important way. How will you know? First, if it's important, you can be fairly well assured that that shall be a topic of discussion in class. Second are the secondary sources such as commercial outlines and canned briefs. If they all go out of their way to highlight a significant point, you can likewise be assured it is important. Finally and bluntly, if you remain awake in class, you'll know.

Hold yourself to a higher standard. While highly organized briefs are not directly a path to success in one of my inns of court, they are an important coincidental indicator. My advisors, barristers, and solicitors seek bright, structured, dedicated minds—as should you strive to make yours thus.

Focus early and consistently on crafting a comprehensive set of outlines, a set of markers for the law. This must be done, and must be done well, for these are the very essence of the law.

Focus early and earnestly on practice exams. Don't cheat. Follow the rules exactly. If the exam is three hours, then take three hours. Take not a two-hour lunch break, or shout to the heavens, *"Nay!* I shall upon a fortnight of cramming know these rules as I know my own flock of she-goats." Were you to find yourself with this attitude before my court, I shall not be amused.

Go forth, learn my laws well and straight; shine bright and true; and be not afraid of creature high or low. No examination shall deter you; no vocational disappointment shall await you. Let no one discourage you; let no further commandment commence with the words "Off with your head!"

> The King
>
> (HRH Thane J. Messinger)
>
> *Law School: Getting In, Getting Good, Getting the Gold*
>
> *The Young Lawyer's Jungle Book: A Survival Guide*

ABOUT THE AUTHOR

Ben Weiss is a graduate of Vanderbilt University and Washington University School of Law.

Weiss received the F. Hodge O' Neal award for the highest grade in corporate law among his graduating class, received an Order of the Barristers distinction for Moot Court, and earned dean's list honors at Washington University School of Law.

After law school, Weiss practiced corporate and securities law for a large firm in the Midwest. He currently resides in New York City. This is his first book.

INDEX

P–Q

R

S

T

U–Z

FOR THE STUDENT

COLLEGE FAST TRACK: ESSENTIAL HABITS FOR LESS STRESS AND MORE
SUCCESS IN COLLEGE,
by Derrick Hibbard
ISBN: 978-1-888960-23-5, 123 pages,
US$12.95

Concise, easy-to-read, and written in an
approachable, peer tone. Focuses on immediately usable habits to help in ways that provide
more—not less—time for enjoyment: success
and less stress. Once college begins, the reading load is heavy (and parties beckon). Thus "extra-curricular" reading is unappealing. *College Fast
Track* offers the *essential* habits for success in college.

LAW SCHOOL FAST TRACK: ESSENTIAL HABITS FOR LAW SCHOOL SUCCESS,
by Derrick Hibbard
ISBN: 978-1-888960-24-2, 93 pages,
US$12.95

For a law student, numerous and massive
assignments loom from the very first day—
with no let-up until final exams—and with
zero feedback until those finals. This book
focuses on the *essential* habits for your very
first week of law school. This book cuts right to the most important
issues. Better success, easier study, and higher grades and graduation
prospects.

LAW SCHOOL UNDERCOVER: A VETERAN PROFESSOR TELLS THE TRUTH
ABOUT ADMISSIONS, CLASSES, CASES, EXAMS, LAW REVIEW AND MORE,
by Professor "X"
ISBN 978-1-888960-15-0, 149 pages,
US$16.95

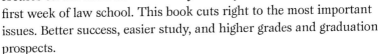

Written by a 20-year veteran law professor, this
book covers the most important aspects of law
school, from selecting the right law school to
admissions to first year to law review, moot
court, and though graduation and jobs. Offers
students the straight truth they will get nowhere else.

THE ART OF THE LAW SCHOOL TRANSFER: A GUIDE TO TRANSFERRING LAW SCHOOLS, By Andrew B. Carrabis and Seth D. Haimovitch
ISBN 978-1-888960-30-3, 160 pg, US$16.95
Transferring from one law school to another is like
painting a panorama. There are the technical elements, sure. Failing to follow these can make colors
sag and smear, destroying all that's done to that
point. In law school, that's a lifetime of academic
preparation. As with all works of art, there's an
artistic element as well. It's not enough to simply
submit papers and files on time. The transfer
process is full of quirks that a novice—any novice—

will not see coming. With this book new students will be prepared, and
will prepare their own works of art. After years of effort and sacrifice,
don't ruin a portrait with needless errors. Instead, create the masterpiece
that will get you into the law school of your dreams.

LATER-IN-LIFE LAWYERS: TIPS FOR THE NON-TRADITIONAL LAW STUDENT,
by Charles Cooper
ISBN 978-1-888960-06-8, 288 pg, US$18.95
Law school is a scary place for any new student.
For an older ("non-traditional") student, it can be
intimidating as well as ill-designed for the needs of
a student with children, mortgages, and the like.
Includes advice on families and children; the LSAT,
GPAs, application process, and law school rankings
for non-traditional students; paying for law school;
surviving first year; non-academic hurdles; and the

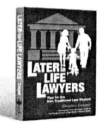

occasional skeleton in the non-traditional closet. This book is a must-
read for the law student who is not going directly from college to law
school.

THE SLACKER'S GUIDE TO LAW SCHOOL: SUCCESS WITHOUT STRESS,
by Juan Doria
ISBN 978-1-888960-52-5, 162 pg, US$16.95
It is easy to fall into a trap of assuming that one
either strives and succeeds or slacks and fails.
Enjoying three years of law school is not the
opposite of learning the law. There's also a
tendency to follow a herd mentality: the
assumption that there's just one right way to do
something, or just one way to study the law. Too
often, this involves too much make-work and too

much stress. This book will show you how to do law school right:
success without stress. (Or at least with *less* stress.)

FOR THE LAW STUDENT

LAW SCHOOL: GETTING IN, GETTING GOOD, GETTING THE GOLD,
by Thane Messinger
ISBN: 978-1-888960-80-8, 367 pages, US$16.95

The key in successful law study is a minimum
of wasted effort and a maximum of results. Still
outlining cases? A waste of time. Failing to use
hypotheticals? A dangerous omission.
Preparing a huge outline? A dangerous waste
of time. Don't waste your time, and don't
neglect what's truly important. Learn law school techniques that work.
Once you're in, Get Good, and Get the Gold!

THE INSIDER'S GUIDE TO GETTING A BIG FIRM JOB: WHAT EVERY LAW
STUDENT SHOULD KNOW ABOUT INTERVIEWING,
by Erika M Finn and Jessica T. Olmon
ISBN-13 978-1-888960-14-3, 130 pages,
US$16.95

The competition for top jobs is intense, and the
special needs of law firm recruiters are
unknown to most law students. Most books
aimed at law students speak to how to get into
law school, and how to succeed in law school, but none address how to
get a lucrative job. This book is an insider's look at the secrets of landing a dream law firm job.

PLANET LAW SCHOOL II: WHAT YOU NEED TO KNOW (BEFORE YOU GO)—
BUT DIDN'T KNOW TO ASK...AND NO ONE ELSE WILL TELL YOU,
by Atticus Falcon
ISBN 978-1-888960-50-7, 858 pages, US$24.95

An encyclopedic reference. Examines hundreds
of sources, and offers in-depth advice on law
courses, materials, methods, study guides, professors, attitude, examsmanship, law review,
internships, research assistantships, clubs, clin-
ics, law jobs, dual degrees, advanced law
degrees, MBE, MPRE, bar review options, and the bar exam. Sets out all
that a law student must master to excel in law school.

JAGGED ROCKS OF WISDOM—NEGOTIATION: MASTERING THE ART OF THE DEAL, by Morten Lund
ISBN: 978-1-888960-09-9, US$15.95
Everyone negotiates. The question is not just whether we negotiate, but whether we negotiate well. In his third book, Morten Lund, a Yale Law graduate and experienced law partner, offers 21 Rules for negotiation skill.

JAGGED ROCKS OF WISDOM: PROFESSIONAL ADVICE FOR THE NEW ATTORNEY, by Morten Lund
ISBN: 978-1-888960-07-5, US$18.95
21 Rules of Law Office Life will help make the difference to your success in the law: surviving your first years as an attorney, and making partner. Beware. Avoid the dangers. Read, read, and read again these 21 Rules of Law Office Life.

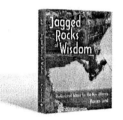

JAGGED ROCKS OF WISDOM—THE MEMO: MASTERING THE LEGAL MEMORANDUM, by Morten Lund
ISBN: 978-1-888960-08-6, US$18.95
Simplifies the most complex aspects of professional work for a new attorney: researching, drafting, and refining the legal memorandum in 21 Rules. In these rules the mysteries are revealed. The process and survival will be no less arduous, but with this book the journey will not be as treacherous.

THE YOUNG LAWYER'S JUNGLE BOOK: A SURVIVAL GUIDE, by Thane Messinger
ISBN 978-1-888960-19-1, US$18.95
Now in its 16th year and second edition, hundreds of sections with advice on law office life, including working with senior attorneys, legal research, memos, contract drafting, mistakes, grammar, email, managing workload, timesheets, annual reviews, teamwork, department, attitude, perspective, and yes, much more.

Recommended in the ABA's *Law Practice Management* and *The Compleat Lawyer,* as well as in numerous state bar journals.